A BLACK MAN
with a
STETHOSCOPE.

A BLACK MAN
with a
STETHOSCOPE.

Racism, Discrimination and
Hatred in the NHS, UK.

for Lisa Brewster,

DR T GORDON FAIR-BRAIN MTETWA, MD

[signature]

XULON PRESS

Xulon Press
2301 Lucien Way #415
Maitland, FL 32751
407.339.4217
www.xulonpress.com

Paperback ISBN-13: 978-1-66282-990-1
Ebook ISBN-13: 978-1-66282-991-8

'A Godly, caring, Doctor, lied to and Betrayed with "50" pieces of "Gold" at an NHS Hospital, UK.

In the United Kingdom, all International Medical Graduates (IMG's) are dehumanized and looked upon as "them" who do not belong. UK does not seem to realize that a lot of medical work is dependent on "them"- BAME.

"BLACK LIVES MATTER"!

TABLE OF CONTENTS

DR T G FAIR-BRAIN'S RAPPORT WITH PATIENTS AND COLLEAGUES

Dr Gordon, as his patients called him, was a hard worker and well-organised person, meticulous, reliable, conscientious, and trustworthy individual. He was also friendly, cheerful with a great sense of humour. He had a good general grounding in the knowledge of General Medicine and

Oncology with the ability to communicate clearly and concisely. We believe he was a highly outgoing individual with a charming personality and an ability to build strong relationships with health colleagues of all levels. He was able to function independently in the clinics and wards even under pressure. He had leadership skills and had the desire to always perform above the status quo. He was very unassuming in his duties, worked well with other colleagues and valued human lives. Finally, we believe he was a good and dependable teamplayer who was firm in his good intentions and beliefs. He respected authority; was able to exercise sound, reasonable and good clinical judgement for the benefit of his patients. He upheld "Good Medical Practice". What might have been said negatively about him had no known evidence to substantiate it.

(The Root)

FOREWORD

This book is dedicated to everyone who is going or has gone through "extreme turbulence" in their life. Maybe, like me, you have screamed, <u>**"I can't breathe"**</u> with nobody responding and have had moments where life seemed meaningless, all hope seemed irretrievable. You may have felt the only option was to throw in the towel.

You do not understand why you were singled out by the enemy to go through what you have experienced or presently experiencing. You are asking questions that no one, seemingly, can answer and the enemy has convinced you that you are cornered for termination and even your God 'cannot save you now'. You feel helpless and hopeless with nowhere to run.

Like everyone else, you are confused and with tears streaming down your cheeks, you are crying out, **"Where are you God when I need you?"** You have heard it said, **God has "No problems, All He has are solutions"** but why can't He solve my problems? I thought He had answers to all problems of life. It appears as if I have been forced to serve time for a crime I did not commit. Day in and day out, nothing has changed for the better. I feel like I am rotting in this spiritual "death row"; time is moving on and there is no noticeable change for the better in my life. You and I know that ONLY GOD can rescue us, and that He does it in His own time and timing.

Like me, your questions are endless; I am still asking today why I have been made a target of "Hatred and Hurt" at this NHS TRUST. I know it is NOT because of anything serious or reprehensible that I committed but because the 'hateful Accusers' have been carefully handpicked by the ENEMY himself to try and terminate one of God's own. Satan trusted these individuals to carry out the job he assigned to them, without question. They were told, "He is **Black**; he **Lacks** and force him to **stay Back**, remember that". These were the special instructions from the enemy. But nothing is permanent in this life even storms cannot go on forever; they must come to an end. In the United (dis-United?) Kingdom, all IMG Blacks are dehumanized and only respected as "they" who do not matter or belong. But UK does not seem to realize that the of health care work force is dependent on "them". "Black Lives Matter"!

(Dr Mtetwa)

INTRODUCTION

According to the dictionary, racism is discrimination or bias based on race. It is believed that a certain race accounts for diversity in human personality or capability and that a certain race is greater and more superior than others. Racism is also described as the belief that inborn different qualities in human racial groups validate discrimination. Modern usage frequently associates racism and racial discrimination and describes the latter term only as wicked practices. Racism is generally associated with actions that are illegal or mostly considered detrimental, such as xenophobia, hatred, extremism, mass murder, self-rule, racial supremacy, terrorism, etc.

Webster's dictionary describes **racism as a conviction that race is the main determinant of human qualities and capabilities, and those racial variances produce an intrinsic superiority or inferiority of a certain racial group.**

Racial discrimination refers to separation of humans through a method of societal division into groupings not necessarily allied to races for purposes of dissimilar treatment. **According to research done at the University of Chicago, it was found that there was prevalent discrimination in the workplaces** against job applicants whose names 'sound black' or sounded "foreign". <u>It is said the GMC in the UK is quick to make harsh and negative decisions on Black professionals whether settled as British citizens or not.</u> These candidates were 50 percent less probable to be considered as compared to those whose names 'sounded white'.

In contrast, organizations and law courts have supported discrimination against whites when it is done to encourage a diverse work or academic environment, even when it was perceived to be to the qualified candidates. These results have been viewed by researchers as strong proof of **unconscious biases deep-rooted in the history of "white" people in Europe or America with the beliefs that they are superior to other races.**

Racism has been a controversial topic for many decades. Is racism the cause for our unjust society? Has racism changed over the years? Research would show that it is worsening, unfortunately. Racism and hatred in the streets, workplaces, football games, in worship places and residential areas is mentioned on an almost daily basis on BBC News in the UK and the world over.

The reality of living in a perfect world is a statement that is far from the truth. Although many of us would like to believe that everyone lives equal lives, that everyone is treated respectfully, and that everyone has equal rights, these aspects are not consistently present in today's society. We live in a diverse world that is separated by race, orientation, and gender. A world where the media defines what makes a person "normal" and what types of people are secluded from society because of what they believe and how they look. In the eyes of God, we are seen as the <u>**Human Race of unique creatures**</u> with our own individuality, however, to others, the sense of being different is often viewed in a negative way. Racism occurs every day in schools, workplaces and in the communities through actions and voices, and occurs intentionally and unintentionally. It can lower a person's self-esteem; often to the point where they may feel that life is not worth living.

Racism could be eliminated if acceptance and equality were present and practiced in our world today. Racism, which can be considered any action or attitude conscious or unconscious, that subordinates an individual or group based on skin colour, or race, is an action that takes three steps to complete.

The first racist action consists of a prejudgment or negative opinion about a group or person. The second is a stereotype or "set image" that is usually based on false information. Finally, the third step of racism is discrimination. Discrimination combines prejudice and stereotype together to create an offensive action that has the "effect of limiting opportunities of certain individuals or groups because of personal characteristics such as race or colour." "All humans belong to the same species, live in the same world and were created equally by God. We were all born with dignity and rights, and we all have the potential to attain a high level of intellectual, social, economic, and cultural development. We are all unique individuals that contribute to the status quo".

Chapter #1

DOES GOD HAVE FAVOURITES?

Those who believe in the God of the Bible must face the question: **Did God create a master race?** Is it the Old Testament Nation of Israel?

From early in the book of Genesis, Scripture follows the forefathers of the nation of Israel, then the nation itself, as well as other nations—as they met Israel. The New Testament follows Spiritual Israel, the Church (see Galatians 6:16), and refers often to Israel, all the way to near the end of its last book (Rev. 21:12).

But does this make the Israelites God's master race? No! God chose Israel as a small nation of slaves, one that was willing to follow Him because of their dire circumstances. He was also keeping a promise to Abraham, grandfather of Israel (Jacob), who faithfully obeyed Him: "**The LORD did not set His love upon you, nor choose you, because you were more in number than any people; for you were the fewest of all people: But**

because the LORD loved you, and because He would keep the oath which He had sworn unto your fathers, has the LORD brought you out with a mighty hand, and redeemed you out of the house of bondmen, from the hand of Pharaoh king of Egypt" (Deut. 7:7-8).

Israel was intended to be a model nation. Ultimately, though, they failed because they did not resist the pulls of the flesh, or the idolatry practiced in neighbouring nations. But in spite of themselves, they proved the point: unless a nation—or person—is converted to a spiritual mindset (Matt. 18:3; Acts 3:19), failure is inevitable.

Root of the Problem

As stated by a columnist in 2001: "Every group needs to know that evil transcends colour, place, politics, sex and religion. It is a universal and recurrent problem we all have to face and fight" (*The New York Daily News*).

Again, no one is immune, either to the effects of racism, or to falling into this mindset themselves. Even the apostle Peter, who was used by Jesus Christ to lead the New Testament Church from AD 31 until his death, felt the effects: "For before that certain came from James, he did eat with the Gentiles: but when they were come, he withdrew and separated himself, fearing them which were of the circumcision. And the other Jews dissembled likewise with him; insomuch that Barnabas also was carried away with their dissimulation. But when I saw that they walked not uprightly according to the truth of the gospel, I said unto Peter before them all, "If you, being a Jew, live after the manner of Gentiles, and not as do the Jews, why compel you the Gentiles to live as do the Jews?" (Gal. 2:12-14).

But **Racism** is only a symptom of a greater problem, not the disease itself. Behind this effect is a cause: human nature is selfish and gravitates toward hatred. It prefers itself, and reflexively dislikes anything that is much different from it. If we think that we are entirely innocent, we deceive ourselves. "The heart is deceitful above all things, and desperately wicked: who can know it?" (Jeremiah 17:9.) This nature must be changed. The good news is that it will be!

Plan for All Races

God is the Creator of all races—yellow, black, and white (with brown and red). Each has strengths and gifts as well as weaknesses.

God's solution for racism has never been to erase the distinctions of the races by intermingling them until there is one homogenized "in-between, not-quite-white/black/yellow" race. This would effectively erase the diversity that He created.

The solution is to enable humanity to unlearn hatred, anger and prejudice, through a real change of heart: "For this is the covenant that I will make with the house of Israel after those days, says the Lord; I will put My laws into their mind, and write them in their hearts: and I will be to them a God, and they shall be to Me a people" (Heb. 8:10).

Those whom God calls to His way of life are unlearning racism now. True Christians "have put on the new man, which is renewed in knowledge after the image of Him that created him: Where there is neither Greek nor Jew...Barbarian [nor] Scythian, bond nor free: but Christ is all, and in all" (Col. 3:10-11).

At a time that is fast approaching, "...there [will] be a highway out of Egypt to Assyria, and the Assyrian shall come into Egypt, and the Egyptian into Assyria, and the Egyptians shall serve with the Assyrians.

"In that day shall Israel be the third with Egypt and with Assyria, even a blessing in the midst of the land: Whom the Lord of hosts shall bless, saying, Blessed be Egypt My People, and Assyria the work of My hands, and Israel Mine inheritance" (Isa. 19:23-25).

Chapter #2

"RACISM"

Racism is the belief that a particular race is superior or inferior to another, that a person's social and moral traits are predetermined by his or her inborn biological characteristics. Racial separatism is the belief, most of the time based on racism, that different races should remain segregated and apart from one another.

Racism has remained pandemic throughout human history. It may be defined as the hatred of one person by another — or the belief that another person is less than human — because of skin color, language, customs, place of birth or any factor that supposedly reveals the basic nature of that person. It has influenced wars, slavery, the formation of nations, and legal codes.

During the past 500-1000 years, racism on the part of Western powers toward non-Westerners has had a far more significant impact on history than any other form of racism (such as racism among Western groups or among Easterners, such as Asians, Africans, and others). The most notorious example of racism by the West has been slavery, particularly the enslavement

5

of Africans in the New World (although slavery itself dates back thousands of years). This enslavement was accomplished because of the racist belief that **Black Africans were less than fully human compared to white Europeans and their descendants.**

This belief was not "automatic": that is, Africans were not originally considered inferior. When Portuguese sailors first explored Africa in the 15th and 16th centuries, they came upon empires and cities as advanced as their own, and they considered Africans to be serious rivals. Over time, though, as African civilizations failed to match the technological advances of Europe, and the major European powers began to plunder the continent and forcibly remove its inhabitants to work as slave laborers in new colonies across the Atlantic, Africans came to be seen as a "deficient species", or as "savages." To an important extent, this view was necessary to justify the slave trade at a time when Western culture had begun to promote individual rights and human equality. The willingness of some Africans to sell other Africans to European slave traders also led to claims of savagery, **based on the false belief that the "dark people" were all kinsmen, all part of one society** — as opposed to many different, sometimes warring nations.

One important feature of racism, especially toward Blacks and immigrant groups, is clear in attitudes regarding slaves and slavery. Jews are usually seen by anti-Semites as subhuman but also superhuman: devilishly cunning, skilled, and powerful. **Blacks and others are seen by racists as merely subhuman, more like beasts than men.** If the focus of anti-Semitism is evil, then the focus of racism is inferiority — directed toward those who have sometimes been considered to lack even the ability to be evil (however, in the 20th century, especially, victims of racism are often considered morally degraded).

In the second half of the 19th century, Darwinism, the decline of Christian belief, and growing immigration were all perceived by many white Westerners as a threat to their cultural control. European and, to a lesser degree, American scientists and philosophers devised a false racial "science" to "prove" the supremacy of non-Jewish whites. While the Nazi annihilation of Jews discredited most of these supposedly scientific efforts to elevate one race over another, small numbers of scientists and social scientists have continued throughout the 20th century to argue the inborn shortcomings of certain races, especially Blacks. At the same time, some public figures in the American Black community have championed the supremacy of their own race and the inferiority of whites—using nearly the identical language of white racists.

All these arguments are based on a false understanding of race; in fact, contemporary scientists are not agreed on whether race is a valid way to classify people. What may seem to be significant "racial" differences to some people — skin color, hair, facial shape — are not of much scientific significance. In fact, genetic differences within a so-called race may be greater than those between races. One philosopher writes: "There are few genetic characteristics to be found in the population of England that are not found in similar proportions in Zaire or in China... those differences that most deeply affect us in our dealings with each other are not to any significant degree biologically determined."

What comes to mind when someone hears the word racism? Many people treat others differently because of their skin colour, which is racism. Racism is wrong in so many ways because people are judging other people who have a darker skin colour than others.

For years before Adolf Hitler became Chancellor of Germany, he was obsessed with ideas about race. In his speeches and writings, Hitler spread his beliefs in racial "purity" and in the superiority for the German Race what was called the Aryan "master race." Hitler and the Nazis are the ones who started the race, he believed.

(http://www.ushmm.org/outreach/en/article.
php?ModuleId=10007679)

The Nazis influenced governments and started training children in school to become racist. They believed that if they eliminated the black people then the whites would overcome them and be in the higher class. In the German eyes back then, different coloured people were considered dirt and were controlled by making them slaves and making them feel worthless. Hitler and other Nazi leaders viewed the Jews not as a religious group, but as a poisonous "race".

Racism is something we have all witnessed. Many people fail to believe that race is not a biological category, but an artificial classification of people with no scientifically verifiable facts. In other words, the distinction we make between races has nothing to do with genetic characteristics. Race was created socially, and primarily by how people perceived ideas and faces with which we lacked familiarity. The definition of race all depends on where and when the word is being used.

In U.S. history, the meaning of the label "white" has changed over time, eventually adding groups like the Italians, Irish and Jews. Other groups, mainly African, Latino, American Indian, Pacific Islander, and Asian descendants, are labelled as "non-white; and have found the path for worldwide social acceptance much more difficult. The irregular boundary of ethnicities touches educational and economic opportunity, political representation, as well as income, health, and social mobility of people of colour.

So where did this type of behaviour begin? There are many ideas about how racism began, however the truth lies in the history of mankind. Before people were able to travel and to experience different groups of people, people predominantly stayed in the same area with the same people. Therefore, each people group feared things that were different and were unable to face the differences. Indeed, travel has changed the isolation we once lived, but the fear never left. **The truth is racism began as soon as people faced those of different races. We have not only, always had the fear of change, but also the fear of the unknown.**

It seems that because racism has been around so long, that we would have been able to overcome it. Even as our species established contact with those whom we fear, it often has led to disputes. The disputes, in time, is what has caused racism to transform from people simply disliking each other, to the permanent and the indestructible foundation of common racism and prejudice.

Contemporary racism is said to have been derived from many places, one of the most common ideas being upbringing. As a child, you are dependent on your parents to help you become who you are to become. Each of our parents have their own distinct opinions. Children do not have their own opinions. Children need the help of their parents, and this is often where the problem starts.

If you were told that all Asians are sneaky, or all Whites are evil, or all Blacks are criminals and thieves, it is likely you will believe it. "Upbringing is the largest cause of racism"-Anon-ymous. Even if we allow ourselves to get to know some of them, this will always be in the back of your mind.

Another suggestion as to how racism makes its way into our heads is through *'the mighty media'*. As we grow up, media becomes a factor of our lives whether we want it to be and is also a major source of how racism keeps itself active. Since the 70's the media has been giving us racist labels. One of the largest sources coming from crime shows like "Law and Order", and "CSI". When dealing with crime, people of colour are reflected in the demarcation of "them" and "us". **Whites are often repre-sented as the "good guys", or the strong, law obeying citizens. They often target people of colour, of the times without any sort of evidence. Directors and writers use racial stereotypes to make a more complex story line.**

In the novel, "The Power of One," by Bryce Courtney, a young, white, African boy named Ricky lived in a time where the gov-ernment, the country, and the world revolved around racism. "World War II is coming to an end, and in South Africa, the whites seem to hate the blacks just as much as the blacks hate the whites. Ricky was raised by a compassionate and loving black woman he refers to as "Nanny", due to the unsafe conditions at home with his bad, mentally ill mother. He grew up with Nanny and his best friend, who was also black. For Ricky, racism did not exist.

A thought on RACISM

Racism is the belief that all members of each race possess characteristics or abilities specific to that race, especially to distinguish it as inferior or superior to another race or races. It is also defined as antagonism against someone. This means that racism can be prejudice, discrimination, or antagonism directed against someone of a different race based on the belief that one's own race is superior. **Racism occurs intentionally and unintentionally. Both are a form of discrimination and dehumanization of the inferior with respect to the popular or superior race.** Again, racial discrimination can be *both*, intentional as well as unintentional; and both are harmful to people and to the culture in which they live. Now one may ask: how can someone unintentionally discriminate against another race? There are quite a few ways. **A major one is traditional upbringing.** The circumstances that people grow up in, have an extremely large impact on their lives, how they handle situations, how they think, and how they talk (and not just in the sense of their accents). In the movie "42" (The Jackie Robinson Story), a heckler in the crowd began shouting vulgar obscenities and racial slurs at Jackie because of his skin, although he was an outstanding ball player. In the movie, the heckler's son was sitting next to him, and began to repeat everything his father was saying. Now, even though this may just be a movie, this is a great representation of how a child's circumstances influence his behaviour. And what one can take away from this scene is that *we* need to be conscious of the example that we set for our kids. As they grow up, they are naturally going to regurgitate what they have heard from their parents. That is simply the way kids were made to learn: by repetition. A parent who is negligent in this aspect of parenting often teach their children to discriminate against other races, whether it be intentional or unintentional. Now that said, there is still a lot of intentional hatred and discrimination even in 2018. A clear demonstration of what happened at the Isle of "Hate and Hurt".

A study reported in The College Student Journal, "The Changing Nature of Racism on College Campuses: Study of Discrimination at a North-eastern Public University" explained that there are a lot of college students that feel the pressure of discrimination even today, although it is less obvious now. The study used three minority groups (**Black, Asian, and Hispanic**) proportionally to the percentage that those minority groups had been represented on the campus. They were asked questions on the topic of racism, and more specifically, if and how they have been affected. As already stated before, the results showed that racism is still a prominent issue. The interesting part is that the longer minority students are on campus, the more likely they are to experience some sort of racially motivated attack, whether it is verbal abuse, physical abuse, or mental abuse.

The author of this book *experienced* verbal, social, emotional, and intellectual abuses at several NHS Hospitals in

the UK, something that is unacceptable or should not be, in this century.

To get rid of racism, we must simply stop talking about it. Now one may think that it is hypocritical to write and talk on the topic of racism and how people need to stop talking about it. But too many people bring up the subject in a manner that has no positive drive to get rid of it. That is the purpose of this book.

Chapter 3

(HATRED)
"A DESTRUCTIVE
FORCE"

EVIL Can be stopped if it cannot be transmuted

"Hatred is Satan masquerading as a shadow of death". To everything there are two poles, or opposite aspects, and those *"opposites"* are really only two extremes of the same thing, with many varying degrees between them.

To illustrate: Heat and Cold, although "opposites," are really the same thing, the differences consisting merely of degrees of the same thing. Look at your thermometer and see if you can discover where "heat" terminates and "cold" begins!

There is no such thing as "absolute heat" or "absolute cold"—the two terms "heat" and "cold" simply indicate varying degrees of the same thing, and that "same thing" which manifests as "heat" and "cold" is merely a form, variety, and rate of Vibration. So "heat" and "cold" are simply the "two poles" one which we call "Heat"—and the phenomena attendant thereupon are manifestations of **the Principle of Polarity.**

The same **Principle** manifests in the case of "**Light and Darkness,**" which are the same thing, the difference consisting of varying degrees between the two poles of the phenomena. Where does "darkness" leave off, and "light" begin? What is the difference between "**Large and Small**"? Between "**Hard and Soft**"? Between "**Black and White**"? Between "**Sharp and Dull**"? Between "**Noise and Quiet**"? Between "**High and Low**"? Between "**Positive and Negative?**"

The Principle of Polarity explains these paradoxes, and no other Principle can supersede it. The same Principle operates on the Mental Plane. Let us take a radical and extreme example—that of "**Love and Hate,**" two mental states apparently totally different. And yet there are degrees of Hate and degrees of Love, and a middle point in which we use the terms "**Like or Dislike,**" which shade into each other so gradually that sometimes we are at a loss to know whether we "like" or "dislike" or "neither." And all are simply degrees of the same thing.

It is possible to change the vibrations of Hate to the vibrations of Love, in one's own mind, and in the minds of others. Many of you, who read these lines, have had personal experiences of the involuntary rapid transition from Love to Hate, and the reverse, in your own case and that of others. **Good and Evil"** are but the poles of the same thing. There is an art of transmuting Evil into Good, by means of an application of the Principle of Polarity.

The "Art of Polarization" becomes a phase of "Mental Alchemy." An understanding of the principle will enable one to change his own Polarity, as well as that of others, if he will devote the time and study necessary to master the art.

Yes— 'HOW'? —I am asking 'YOU'... Any good answers? — besides the usual.

"Just let go of the hate... let it go..." or "meditate and imagine only good thoughts..."

'HATE' is of the dark forces— and it's a little harder to get rid of than simply meditating or wishing it away... especially when the factor behind the hate; (usually a person or persons) do not 'apologize' for their ill behaviour.

Usually, these individuals repeat the cycle that was ingrained in them; being treated badly without being apologized to... and it's rampant among the selfish ones of the world, who, not by accident, make up the ruling elite, such as the "the rich & famous" … and, thus, you have the premise for the "ills of the world"

In some cases, hatred for someone is something that is rather impossible to erase, and in most cases, it's something that may feel intensely painful, unnatural, and unjust to even 'Try' to erase.

But **hatred is toxic and destructive by nature to everyone exposed to it,** and whether the object of your hatred deserves all the hate and resentment you feel for them, you do not deserve to be exposed to it.

Hatred to some extent is a necessary human emotion, it can fuel people to do things that can result in "Justice". But once that concept of justice has been carried to a certain extent and burnt itself out, it's important to let go of the hatred that fuelled it, because after that point, all the destructive energy of that hatred and resentment can only be directed inward, and/or towards people who don't truly deserve it.

The way I see it, if someone has done something that makes you hate them, and if they feel no remorse for it, then they must want to cause you pain. So, past a certain point, the worst thing you can do to them, and more importantly, the best thing you can do for yourself, is to let go of all emotion for them and stop letting them cause you yet more pain by hating them.

Yes, I do believe that if you harbour hate it will poison you. Hate is insidious and sneaky. It hides in the hidden chambers of your heart until it festers and takes over completely. Just a little hate can infect your whole being before you are even aware it has taken root. Hate must be banished as soon as you feel it is first pangs in your heart. It will destroy you.

This year (2020) I learned about "neutral acknowledgements" and it is helpful in conjunction with meditation. For example, a thought against someone arises in my mind/emotions and instead of pushing it away or rationalizing it or stewing in it I look at it and acknowledge it ("I acknowledge that I feel anger towards racists) and I try to be very specific and I may have to work on it a few times to get to the specificity of the negative emotion. I don't want to make it sound like it is easy at first, but it comes with practice.

Sometimes I must go and look at my life to get to the root of my negativity towards someone, my workmate for example. There are plenty of people who can help you look at a moment in the past. For an example, I have felt emotions of hate arise towards whites who threw me out of a restaurant in Rhodesia because I was black. After careful thought I realize that a human being evolves. Who I was is quite different from who I am today.

Also, if you are actively processing someone using one of the basic psychotechnology's (a big word, I know) you will gradually get the realization that *all people are basically good*, just that they have had a lot of past life trauma and they did not always behave nobly and **they need to forgive themselves and drop the toxic energy with their self-defeating and destructive messages.**

Also, as you have more past life dramas related to you in session you will start to get some idea of our recent cosmic history (and not so recent) and you will start to see that what really got us into trouble was our consistent refusal to forgive and love and understand and instead devise all kinds of punishments and controls. And here we are, **the good and the bad, we are all in the same boat now.**

I think that is what Jesus meant when he said that if you live by the sword you will die by the sword. The inventor of the guillotine should have taken heed.

Most people just accept that there will always be crime and hatred. and so, a great process of busyness and emotional numbing just to survive where they live or what is going on in the world. **People have just become adjusted to crime and living with hate.**

I would like to ask the opposite question to this: how can we get people adjusted to living with peace, love and the reality of spirit or soul? What can we do or think or believe in a unified way to bring this about?

Any good answers? —besides the usual; "just let go of the hate... let it go..." or, "meditate and imagine only good thoughts..."

'Hatred' is of the dark forces— and it's a little harder to get rid of than simply meditating or wishing it away... especially when the factor behind the hate; (usually a person or persons) do not 'apologize' for their ill behaviour.

Usually, these individuals repeat the cycle that was ingrained in them; being treated badly without being apologized to... and it's rampant among the selfish ones of the world, who, not by accident, make up the ruling elite, such as the "Jones's"... and, thus, you have the premise for the "ills of the world". Here, below, are some comments on the characterization of the problem but unfortunately, the 'solutions' are hard to come by:

I believe that we intuitively understand that individuals whose lives are consumed with hatred of others live shallow, pitiful, and ultimately self-destructive ones.

History has shown that even societies whose past was notable for tremendous cultural and scientific progress can plummet to the depth's suicidal self-annihilation when their fanatical goal is genocide—witness Nazi Germany in the 20th century.

<u>Hatred is a karmic cancer</u> whose victim is its perpetrator. It is a spiritual black hole that consumes those who are obsessed with it.

Unfortunately, we can see the consequences of such attitudes in some parts of the Muslim world today. Hatred of "nonbelievers: of the West, of America and especially of Israel" is such an all-consuming fact of life that there is energy for little else.

How is it possible to develop a civil society based on principles of liberty and free expression (formerly a basic tenet of leftist doctrine) when religious fanaticism blocks any dissent? How can, at least, half of the population (women) be subjugated and regarded as chattel. Where is the energy to create works of art, of music, of philosophy, literature? And what about science and medicine? **What about the development of advances that can help ALL humanity?** The irony is that the Muslim world was such a leader–in philosophy, art, science. That was about 500 years ago. But apparently such a worldly approach was compatible with its religious tenets then. Is it not true now, in the 21st century?

Yes, to my leftist friends–Israel is militarily superior to the Palestinians. And yes, there are legitimate reasons for Palestinian frustration with their political conditions and standard of living.

Attacking their more powerful neighbour, knowing their own civilians will be killed when they hide their weapons among them is clearly self-destructive. And to my leftist friends–is hatred and targeting of civilians a strategy to laud? Is religious intolerance and genocidal rhetoric now a part of the world's leftist creed?

The thrill of killing another human being is a spiritual poison– regardless of the impetus for doing so. Examples today: the infamous ISIS or the Boka Haram. Former prime minister Golda Meir is quoted as saying "there will not be peace between Israel and the Arabs (substitute Islam and the West) until Arab mothers love their children more than they hate us." I would prefer to put it this way, "until the white father/mother learns to love his/her black son-in-law". It is a powerful yet sad statement. Of course, white fathers/mothers love their children. So why do they feed their children a diet of fanatical hatred? This is so poisonous in some homes that even white preachers are not spared. One white preacher is known to have to quote the Scriptures erroneously, that it was against God's intentions and plans that a black man marries a white lady. This is unscriptural.

Societies driven by hatred take on the karmic burden that individuals do–they will ultimately fail. They will succumb to the karmic poison, the darkest of energies known to the universe. It is an interesting point that Hatred is becoming a thought crime, and I agree with that point.

I also agree that the ruling elite is only concerned with the continuation of their control over the masses (encompassing individuals of all colours, beliefs, etc.) and will outlaw Hate or Thought or anything else that they feel they must be persecuted to hold onto their control. I think it is extremely tragic that most people accept, without questioning, the measures that their ruling elite implements to control them (such as gun control) automatically assuming that these measures are designed to benefit them–an assumption that makes zero sense.

Democracy is a fraud which is based on two false assumptions:

1–people elect the government that will best work for them

2–this government works tirelessly for the benefit of the people which elected it.

These two false assumptions make perfect sense to the masses because they fit in with each other so perfectly. 2 follows out of 1 and 1 follows out of 2. the only problem is that both 1 and 2 are purely imaginary and the fact that they do not contradict each other means absolutely nothing for the pesky thing called reality.

And I would have still believed this lie if not for one messed up–international policy. **International policy is based on the idea that the government must lie to its own people for their own benefit.** This is contrary to the main two false assumptions which say that people reward politicians by re-electing them. How can a politician be rewarded for something he did secretly? How can you elect a politician that is best for you when his intentions are secret from you? The answer is very simple–you never do elect politicians that are best for you, and they never do work in your interests whether they act secretly or not–they always work in their own interests as does everybody else. Unfortunately, the majority of those who vote do not understand this. Most of the times when these politicians are running for office, they promise the moon to the people and yet all they are doing is looking to satisfy number One – "I, Me and Myself". Very few ever care for the welfare of the people.

The Human Race

Against <u>Racism</u>, Against <u>Hatred</u>

The belief that all members, of each race, possess characteristics, abilities, or qualities specific to that race, especially so as to distinguish it as inferior or superior to another race or races: theories of racism. (The definition of racism, Oxford Dictionary)

Take a moment to think back to your school days and see if you remember an incident when someone you knew was <u>racially mocked</u>. Most likely you do – maybe it was a gesture, a joke or even a physical attack. The reality is that this type of bullying can affect the life and self-esteem of the victim for the rest of their life. The author of this book, for the rest of his life, will be affected by the racially motivated mistreatment received at the Isle of Wight in the UK. Yes! He can forgive or has forgiven the people who purposely attempted to derail him, but he cannot forget the Evil intent that was in it. Forgiving is easy but forgetting and trusting again is sometimes impossible though we always say, "Forgive and Forget".

"A child is not born with Racism; it is taught"

But this behaviour does not stop with children but continues into adulthood with many people. The "Independent" recently highlighted a shocking poll which revealed that **1 in 3 Brits had thoughts and feelings which would be considered as racist.** What's alarming is that previous such reports have suggested that many people's feelings of hostility towards foreigners was passed down from previous generations.

This might seem obvious, since *we know that racism isn't genetic, so it must be taught.* Just like a child is taught manners, morals or right from wrong, a parent or carer can nurture feelings of racial resentment in a child. You may have witnessed young children in playgrounds. Children are too young to be tainted by such nurturing. When left with other children of a different colour, they will happily play together, as naturally as they would with children of their own colour. For such children, **colour does not come into the equation–because racism is not part of their natural disposition.**

Most people may think that we have moved into the 21st century without the racial tensions and prejudices that have plagued our world in the past. Following the victory of the second world war in the 40's, the U.S. Civil Rights Movements of the 60's, the disintegration of past apartheid states in the 90's, and the appointment of a black U.S. president in the new century, we do see greater integration in the world today…but <u>the disease of racism</u> continues to dwell amongst us, as many will testify:

It is an unerasable pandemic that has survived generations. "Racism is still with us. But it is up to us to prepare our children for what they have to meet, and, hopefully, we shall overcome." Rosa Parks, American Civil Rights Activist and many Innocent People Who Suffered for Crimes they did not commit.

It is something that most of us can only imagine in our darkest nightmares. Being arrested or vilified by the press for a crime that you did not commit. It is the stuff of Academy Award–winning dramas and "Franz Kafka novels". It is also something that happens more often than we would like to think.

Quite a few people from the black community in America are quoted. The one thing they all had in common was that they were black, and the system conspired to make them appear guilty of a terrible crime they had nothing to do with. Think it could not happen to you? Maybe not in a physical "death row" but **Dr Fair-Brain was placed in an "Emotional death row" by the General Medical Council of the United Kingdom.** Here are several examples of "emotional death row":

<u>Example #1</u> ~In the 60's, seven blacks (Civil Rights Activists) stopped to eat at a restaurant when Law Enforcement Officers

A Black Man with a Stethoscope.

in the USA forced them to leave, but all they did was stop to eat something. They had caused no problem in the restaurant, yet they were arrested and jailed. The humiliation did not end with unlawful arrest; for they all received severe beatings.

After this brutal attack they were locked up behind bars. While behind bars, they remembered what happened to Paul and Silas when they were thrown in jail after receiving severe beatings. Paul and Silas were imprisoned for telling others about Jesus. This did not dampen their spirits; about midnight they were praying and singing hymns to God. "Who, having received such a charge, thrust them into the inner prison, and made their feet fast in the stocks." (Acts 16:25).

Is being black a curse or a sin? Why do you allow such atrocities, Oh God? One of the actors of the twentieth century, Sidney Portiere once said, "everywhere he went the main thing that preceded him was his black colour…"

Example #2 ~Dr Fair-Brain was sold a hamburger and a milk shake and was told to go and eat outside the restaurant, by the white owner of the restaurant, in his own country of birth, before the end of the Smith regime in Rhodesia now called Zimbabwe.

Example #3 ~ In South Africa, Dr Fair-Brain was asked to join the que "for black people Only at a bank because he was standing in a que for "whites only". Of course, this was before the dismantling of the Apartheid Policy in South Africa.

<u>Example #4</u> ~ In Grayson, Kentucky, USA, he was at Kentucky Christian College when **two "white men"** from Mississippi came into Grayson and wanted to beat him up at a Pizza place because **he was black.** They claimed that they had been beaten in Mississippi by black men so, they wanted to beat him too. But what had that to do with him, a young man in Grayson, Kentucky, USA all the way from Africa. He was rescued by his friends from Bible College who would not allow that to happen.

The Shadow

Dr Fair-Brain's guilt of blackness kept following him like a ghost, because everywhere he went because (even years later) he had to face the same racial bias at the Isle of Wight for being a black doctor, since he was not accepted by <u>"two white nurses"</u> in the Acute Oncology Department where only the white colour was accepted. The "white people" compiled false allegations to get him removed from the St Mary's Hospital as an incompetent doctor but "the real reason was because **he was Black and of African origin".** He had 'No Clinical issues though the GMC tried its best to manufacture some when they were invited to investigate. He never lost a patient from clinical carelessness or by some unforeseen problems beyond his ability. He worked well with all medical staff of all levels for the 15 years he had worked in both private sector and NHS in the UK since 2001.

After the 'partial hearing' by the **'White Disciplinary Committee' of the St Mary's NHS TRUST Hospital,** he was reported to the wicked and manipulative General Medical Council of the United Kingdom, whose verdict (after a lengthy and unfair investigation) was an **"Emotional and Financial Death Row"** for Dr Fair-Brain from which ONLY God Almighty could rescue him. His License to practice medicine was revoked, and he lost his job. He could not practice medicine anywhere in the world. He was declared "A risk to the public and patients and a disgrace to medicine" and NOT for clinical malpractice but **the same guilt of Blackness dogged him everywhere he went – South Africa, Rhodesia, America, and the United Kingdom – hence Racism still pandemic as well.**

He was destroyed financially and was reduced to one meal a day before receiving food from his church. This was food being thrown away by the Tesco's and other big grocery stores. Foods whose dates of use had expired (see photos below 2016 to 2018). Dr Fair-Brain could not understand why God allowed this to happen to His own.

"The Wicked Will Be Punished"

"Evil shall slay the wicked, and those who hate the righteous will be condemned." (Psalm 34:21)

God makes clear in His Word what the end of the wicked will be. Their punishment is inescapable: "Those who hate the righteous will be condemned." This is a basic characteristic of the nature of God. He must punish evil. In His self-revelation to Moses in Exodus 34:6-7, God proclaimed the fundamental qualities of His nature: **"compassionate, gracious, slow to anger, abounding in lovingkindness ... yet who will by no means leave the guilty unpunished ... "**. God reveals here that the punishment of evil is part of His innate nature. We need not wonder if it will be done, or if the wicked will not suffer for their wrongs. As surely as God, and this universe, exists, the wicked will be judged. Nothing is more certain in the universe. **The God of justice will punish evil.**

Presidents may posture and say after a terror attack: "These perpetrators will be found and brought to justice" — but the truth is, they may or may not be able to find and punish the evildoers. But no one can hide from God. He sees every hiding place. And He WILL bring the guilt of every soul to punishment. This is just to remind you that you cannot hide from God. He will find you, and you will pay for your sins.

More pertinent to us is that He will do this not only for the "terrorist" or those committing what we consider to be "great atrocities", but for the sins of each of us! How shall we escape **the certain judgment of God which we rightly deserve?** The thought of facing His certain judgment should terrify us, and it should cause us to seek refuge from the Messiah, for He graciously provided atonement bearing the punishment for our sins!

So, racism still exists in societies today. Maybe it is more hidden and subtle, but the effects of it are still present, requiring us to educate ourselves on how to deal with it. So, please join 'Against Racism'.

As one famous man once said; "To me the earth's most explosive and pernicious evil is racism, the inability of God's creatures to live as One, especially in the Western world." (Malcolm X–El-Hajj Malik El-Shabazz). Dr Martin Luther King said, "mankind has been able to conquer space, and even get man to the moon; but yet still cannot learn to live together."

Islam's Stance Against Racism

There are many groups and individuals that still hold abhorrent views of other people who are of a different race or caste. An arrogant hatred stemming from feelings of racial superiority. We, as Muslims, are calling people to stand up against such views, whether held within our circle of friends, families, colleagues, or communities–'Against Racism, Against Hatred'.

Islam's View on Racism

Islam teaches that all people are equal and the only difference between people is their level of piety and God consciousness.

In the Qur'an, it clearly states: *"Oh Mankind,* We (God) created you from a single pair of a male and a female (Adam and Eve), and made you into tribes and nations so that you may know one another (not so that you despise each other). Verily, the most honoured of you in the sight of Allah (God) is he who is most righteous of you." (The Qur'an, Chapter 49, Verse 13)

So, all humans descend from Adam and Eve. In that sense, we are all essentially brothers and sisters. Our differing colours and diversity are not there to cause division, but as a method of recognising one another. Such traits do not elevate a person's status but rather our status with God is based on our level of piety and righteousness. I was not better than my brothers because I was lighter in colour than others; I was just a different shade compared to them.

Unfortunately, a white colour is still supposed to be status-elevating to the point of treating the different colours as inferior; this happens even in the Judeo-liturgical environments. Dr T G Fair-Brain was clearly segregated at one of the Judeo-Christian Fellowship he was attending despite being a professional individual.

In a further verse from the Qur'an: "And amongst his signs is the creation of heaven and the earth, and the diversity of your language and colours; Verily, in these are signs for those who have knowledge." (The Qur'an, Chapter 30, Verse 22)

The Prophet Muhammad is authentically reported to have said: "Allah does not look at your appearances or wealth but looks at your actions". The Christian Bible says, "Do not consider his appearance or his height, for I have rejected him. The LORD does not look at things people look at. People look at the outward appearance, but the LORD looks at the heart" (1 Samuel 16:7).

The Prophet (phub) also reiterated this point in his last sermon to the people, as can be seen from the following excerpt:

"O people remember that your Lord is One. An Arab has no superiority over a non-Arab nor a non-Arab has any superiority over an Arab; also, a black has no superiority over white, nor a white has any superiority over black, except by piety and good action (Taqwa). Indeed, the best among you is the one with the best character (Taqwa). (The Prophet's Last Sermon as reported in Baihaqi)

As can be seen from the above quote, Islam is the antidote to racism, since in Islam there is no tolerance for racism. Muslims feel it is a duty to convey these messages within our wider society and work towards the common good, both in word and deed.

Malcolm X's Letter from Hajj

Islam also promotes racial integration through its practices. For example, the Islamic Hajj (pilgrimage to the first house of worship built by Abraham–the Kaaba), which takes place every year, is attended by millions of people of different races and colours. As in other Islamic practices, it encourages people to mix freely together in performing the pilgrimage rites and to pray side by side as one community.

Through such unity, the pilgrimage can have a profound effect on people. One such example of this was in 1967, when Malcolm X travelled to Saudi Arabia for the Hajj. At the time, Malcolm X was still considered a black supremacist. By the time of his pilgrimage to Mecca, Malcolm X was no longer a member of the Nation of Islam (NOI). NOI is a black-racist group established in 1950's America but has no ties or resemblance to orthodox Islam (elements of orthodox Islam were practised by the group, but others were developed by its leader who was a former convict and self-proclaimed prophet).

On travelling to Mecca, Malcolm X was astounded at the racial integration and the racial equality that he witnessed. He had never experienced these elsewhere. Here is an excerpt of a letter from Malcolm X after he attended the hajj in 1967:

"There were tens of thousands of pilgrims, from all over the world. They were of all colours, from blue-eyed blondes to black-skinned Africans. But we were all participating in the same ritual, displaying a spirit of unity and brotherhood that my experiences in America had led me to believe never could exist between the white and non-white."

"America needs to understand Islam, because this is the one religion that erases from its society the race problem. Throughout my travels in the Muslim world, I have met, talked to, and even eaten with people who in America would have been considered white—but the white attitude was removed from their minds by the religion of Islam. I have never before seen sincere and true brotherhood practiced by all colours together, irrespective of their colour."

"During the past eleven days here in the Muslim world, I have eaten from the same plate, drunk from the same glass, and slept on the same rug–while praying to the same God–with fellow Muslims, whose eyes were the bluest of blue, whose hair was the blondest of blond, and whose skin was the whitest of white. And in the words and in the deeds of the white Muslims, I felt the same sincerity that I felt among the black African Muslims of Nigeria, Sudan and Ghana."

"We were truly all the same (brothers)–because their belief in one God had removed the white from their minds, the white from their behaviour, and the white from their attitude."

Al-Hajj Malik El-Shabazz (Malcolm X) (On returning from hajj, Malcolm X became a Muslim). Dr Fair-Brain is mentioning and making all these quotes from the Islamic practices to make a point.

Chapter # 4

RACISM AND HATRED IN THE UK-NHS

Racism in selection, training, and employment of doctors

Alongside the newly promoted 'hostile environment' other forms of racism continue in the NHS. A recent blog in the BMJ recalled that data from the late 1980s suggested that BME doctors were six times less likely to obtain hospital jobs than their white counterparts with identical qualifications, while in the 1990s, both a national study and one focusing on London medical schools found that BME applicants were less likely to be selected than their white counterparts. More recently, there has been much controversy regarding potential racial biases in assessment of doctors, such as the MRCGP postgraduate exams. Despite these historical findings, there has been no robust contemporary research on these issues.

Many doctors have expressed belief that BME doctors are subject to much harsher treatment in disciplinary procedures compared with white staff. In a recent high-profile case, Dr

Bawa Garba was convicted of manslaughter and struck from the GMC register following the death of a child. The case led to a UK-wide outcry from medical staff who point out that the death, albeit tragic, was the result of a single error made by a paediatrician with an otherwise excellent record in a significantly understaffed and busy service and against a background of many system failures.

For instance, in a BMJ comment, a consultant cardiologist contrasted Dr Bawa-Garba's harsh treatment with the 'GMC's leniency when dealing with doctors whose conduct is more worrying. **The GMC took no action against 100 doctors placed on the Sex Offenders Register (SOR) for accessing child pornography–they remained on the Medical Register without even the requirement to inform their patients that they were on the SOR.** The GMC allowed a consultant gynaecologist to remain on the Medical Register without restrictions when he was placed on the SOR. **The GMC allowed doctors to remain on or return to the Medical Register after a period of suspension: after one performed inappropriate private surgery, including total colectomy, for personal gain; after one gave desperate patients with cancer expensive private treatments that have no scientific basis; after several defrauded charities and medical insurance companies, and a doctor who appeared before two separate Fitness to Practise Panels that found that he repeatedly committed research misconduct'.**

The author (Black-British) of this book has been erased after working in the UK after >12 years of working as a doctor with **no clinical issues; never appeared before any disciplinary committee for malpractice and never lost a patient carelessly** or by unavoidable circumstances, but ONLY One strike was enough to throw him out. He was also **falsely accused by** <u>Two</u> <u>White Nurses</u> **who did not like a Black doctor in charge of them.** More details are discussed in the next chapter of the book.

The GMC should deal forcefully with doctors that are deliberately and repeatedly dishonest rather than conscientious doctors who make genuine and single clinical errors. (Dr Fair-Brain made no clinical error, <u>he just happened to be</u> <u>BLACK which was guilty enough for the GMC.</u>)

Other racial experiences by NHS staff.

A 2014 National Health Executive report, "The Snowy White Peaks of the NHS" survey of staff found, that *BME* staff were treated less favourably than white staff in recruitment, including boards, access to career development, disciplinary processes, were bullied more, and were victimised more seriously if they were whistle-blowers. A 2015 survey of every NHS trust showed that 75 percent of acute trusts found a higher percentage of BME staff being harassed, bullied, or abused by staff compared to white staff. In 86 percent of acute trusts, BME staff felt that their organisation did not offer equal opportunities for career progression or promotion.

The political and social discord thrown up by Brexit has meant the status of, and attitudes towards, overseas doctors and medical students has received renewed focus. A 2017 BMA survey of over 3,000 doctors found that almost half of those who qualified outside the EU feel patients treat them differently.

- A January 2018 Pulse survey of GPs found that three quarters of all BME respondents had faced racial discrimination from patients at some point, with more than a quarter of BME GPs report experiencing discrimination from patients at least monthly, with some reporting that it is a daily occurrence.

Challenging racism in the NHS

These examples show that racism is alive and plays a prominent role in the NHS – and takes many forms. Campaigners seek an NHS which provides comprehensive care to everyone in need in the UK and is free for all patients. We need NHS staff at every level who feel valued and who do not experience racism and discrimination either from their own institutions and professional bodies or from patients. We seek government policies that support this, and an end to the individual and institutional racism described above. Every small thing done to get rid of Racism will help towards its elimination. I personally admired what the Arizona, Cardinals' helmets show on the posterior part: <u>"End Racism"</u> or <u>"Inspire Change".</u> Any small thing everyone does to bring about the awareness of sick and tired everyone is of the Racism and Hatred.

Chapter #5

EMPLOYMENT–HATRED AND RACISM AT THE IoW TRUST

D r G. Fair-Brain was hired as a Specialty Doctor in Medical Oncology at the Isle of Wight from December 2013. Two to three months later he was dragged unceremoniously through one of the most shocking Investigations by the Isle of "White" "<u>White</u>" Disciplinary Panel. The panel included the Chief Medical Officer (CMO), Human Resources Head (HR) and the Clinical Director (CD). Dr T.G. Fair-Brain was found guilty of some Racial <u>(Black)</u> and False Allegations.

<u>The Allegations were:</u>

1) **Clinical Incompetence as a doctor as decided by <u>Two White Nurses.</u>** Eight patients privately recorded by the "White" Clinical Nurse Specialist (CNS) were said to have been incorrectly examined, claimed the CNS-JB. Patients

were later examined by other doctors and nothing wrong was confirmed; in fact, they concurred with Dr Fair-Brain. This allegation was taken off the list later when reported to the GMC, so for what was the doctor found guilty?

2) **He was accused of lying to the Appraiser** because he did NOT volunteer information that he had been investigated before at the Royal Derby Hospital. He was NOT being investigated at the time of his appraisal with the Appraiser, and that was why he told the Appraiser he was not under investigation. The Appraiser's poorly communicated question, in the English language, was inquiring on any investigations pending and he said, "None". The doctor later apologised to put out a small fire that he thought would have burnt out of control if he did not give in quickly. He did not feel like he was even supposed to apologise about it but to show respect; he agreed he misunderstood, and it was **Dr Fair-Brain's fault but still that was not enough.**

3) The doctor was accused of NOT completing his Mandatory Training but had completed the training assigned by the Asst. General Manager, (MB); who later added some more topics after the doctor had long finished the ones assigned. The doctor's wife was there and could vouch for this. They later discovered that the AGM was out of line harassing a doctor about completion of Mandatory Training topics. **It was NOT within her scope of duty to oversee and harass the doctor over the Mandatory Training.**

The question was: what exactly was the doctor being investigated for? To be honest, he still is not sure, even today, why he has been put through what he went through the past 6 years from the Isle of Wight and later by the "Competent GMC". He was taken through the Disciplinary Panel which upheld the fabricated allegations. What is amazing is that he had been found guilty of something else other than the original allegations. What was presented to the Disciplinary Panel and eventually sent to the GMC were different allegations. Incompetence was left out, so his Blackness was the main (unmentioned) reason because they could NOT state one substantial reason. The "white" nurses did not like him around their office despite the dog's smiles.

May it be pointed out also that after ONLY two or three months, the two nurses, supported by the TRUST, decided the new doctor was guilty of "clinical incompetence though there was nothing to show for the accusation? Two nurses, the Asst. General Manager, and the irresponsible Officer convinced the Trust that Dr Fair-Brain Mtetwa was not good enough. This was after ONLY two months of being at the institution while still finding his way around. No! He was not the Right colour, that was the undisputable fact. There was clear Institutional Racism condoned by the Trust.

The Clinical Director for AOS (MN) was not even aware of Dr Fair-Brain being harassed by the nurses and it is doubtful whether he genuinely cared to be aware, anyway. Nothing had been reported to him about the doctor's incompetence. He had never been contacted about the doctor's work before sending him to the Disciplinary Committee of the Trust. Nothing was reported to him about him during the two-months of work there.

The two nurses were NOT happy with the doctor being in the same office with them. Why? It is not clear why NOT. **Maybe he was too Black for them.** Truly, they showed plastic smiles every day, but it appeared they did NOT trust the doctor being in the same office with them. We could only speculate reasonably that it was his God-given Colour which was NOT acceptable in their presence. One reason for saying that is because of the temptations he was put through.

Pound coins

"Testing the doctor to see if he was a thief"

The Chemotherapy Sister, **one of the two "White" nurses, left pound coins maybe up to 50 or more on her table to see if the doctor would steal some of them.** The doctor was always the last one to leave the office. Nothing happened to her money. And about two weeks later the other "White" CNS, **who was struggling with money at home herself, also left about the** same amount of pound coins on her table overnight. But again, the doctor did not touch the coins. This behaviour not only disturbed the doctor, but also hurt his pride. The doctor had been left to imagine that they would think so lowly of him. It was as if they felt he stole his way through life in order to get to where he was.

This was mentioned to **the Trust and the General Medical Council (GMC)**, but nothing was done about the incidents. They told him to write a formal report but were quite indifferent about it. The Trust did not feel it was serious enough to make effort to stamp out such racism and hatred.

The GMC claimed they had to investigate the doctor for more than 4 years; what exactly were they investigating; he could not say? Anything positive and respectable about the doctor was purposely left out of the investigation's findings. Any supportive consultants for doctor were left out and considered hostile witness because "the Caring and Efficient GMC" was working on derailing the doctor to please the Trust.

About work, he had <u>ONLY</u> worked about fourteen months in the last four years (fifty-two months). At the last two Trusts, patients wrote very pleasant letters about Dr Fair-Brain and the TRUSTS wanted to hire him on a permanent basis, and yet the Nurses at the Isle of Wight convinced their TRUST he was incompetent. It does not take rocket science to figure out that Dr Fair-Brain was treated the way he was because of something more than <u>the alleged incompetence</u>. The doctor has "Protected Characteristics" – **Black, of African origin and** of a faith different from theirs (if they had any*).* He was a target for gross racism and hatred.

The behaviour of the Isle of Wight Trust demonstrated nothing but a behaviour of "**Institutional Racism**" is a behaviour that should be erased from government institutions. If it were a 'white' doctor treated as he had been, something to the doctor's benefit would have been done; and, most likely nothing would not have been reported to the Disciplinary Panel of the Trust and the GMC.

For the last seven years, Dr T G Fair-Brain, suffered unimaginable stress, anxiety, social deprivation, emotional trauma, occasional physical ailments, intellectual stalemate, financial destitution, and spiritual depression. He is still experiencing Post Traumatic Stress Disorder (PTSD)Physically, Socially, Intellectually, Emotionally and Spiritually) to this day.

This was gross travesty of fundamental human rights in today's civilized society. Racism is a breach of and against the British values of democracy, or so I have been led to believe.

The following is very confidential letter by **one consultant observer,** that the doctor talked to about his treatment at the Isle of Wight Trust and he could not help but reveal his own observations of the department and the lack of respect and trust for Doctor Fair-brain, a very unfortunate and sorry situation for the doctor.

"Letter of Revelation"

Dr. S.

Dr T G Fair-Brain has asked me to write you briefly to support his application to the WR. It appears his situation is being unfairly represented by some of our offices from the Hospital here. Dr Fair-Brain has been with us at the St Mary's Hospital for over 8 months now. We all seemed pleased when we heard about the arrival of the <u>new Specialty Doctor to join the Oncology department.</u>

I recall the Lead Nurse in Oncology expressing her delight after hearing how <u>he seemed to be quite capable and getting along well with the junior doctors in the wards, A&E and MAU</u> where he did his ward rounds. We met occasionally with Dr Fair-Brain in Urology MDTs. I found him <u>a very pleasant and well-informed physician</u> in his department.

Unfortunately, we have had unsatisfactory leadership in the Oncology Department which Dr Fair-Brain has faced as well. This unfortunately has made us lose many Specialty Doctors who have tried to join the department. This is regrettable, and the problem will persist until the TRUST corrects <u>the root of the problem.</u>

The nursing staff in the chemotherapy seem to compound the problem as well because <u>they seem to get away with interfering with doctors joining the Oncology Department</u> as if competing for authority which should not be the case. <u>I have had problem myself working with the Nursing Sister in charge of Chemotherapy;</u> she started acting like she knew better than I. <u>I can relate to Dr Fair-Brain's difficulties dealing with the personnel there.</u>

I was just about to do his Appraisal in September but will allow you at the WR to handle it. He told me he had written to the GMC to let them know he would not be ready for re-validation this coming November because there was interference while he was working on his patients and colleague contacts and the three hundred sixty instructions in preparations for the Re-validation.

<u>He was investigated recently when the Oncology Nursing Staff made some false allegations about his work, which was not substantiated. There seem to be "some racial issues" for which I should not be quoted, but it has nothing to do with his work competence.</u>

He has shown me the transfer letter sent by our Chief Medical Officer – <u>Dr P, whose comments, I feel are very unfair</u>. The medical officer was mistreated by his department for reasons which are not clear to us all, and therefore should not be the one receiving such damning and nasty information.

You interviewed Dr Fair-Brain and you were interested in hiring him. <u>I would not deny him the opportunity.</u> He is joining you as a locum for six months or longer; you will find how he functions. I just have a feeling you will not be disappointed. He has been working unfortunately with the wrong people, at the wrong time. In my opinion, you should hire him.

Please feel free to contact me if there is anything, I can help clarify for you about this gentleman.

Yours sincerely,

T Mosley

Dr Thurmond Mosley (Of course, the GMC was Not interested in the testimony of this consultant because they were in search of something <u>negative and nefarious</u>)

You hated me so much you had to lie about me. I will NOT HATE you but will, instead, forgive you.

Chapter #6

"MOBBING" IN A WORKPLACE TO "EMOTIONAL & PHYSICAL ABUSE".

(This is what Dr T. G Fair-Brain was exposed to at the St Mary's Hospital. The doctor actually experienced everything pointed out in this article. It is the responsibility of the involved Organisation or TRUST to investigate and put an end to such problems. For Doctor Fair-Brain, Racism seems to stand out as the aetiology of the false and hateful Allegations against him at the Hospital. Unfortunately, no in-depth investigation was carried out by the authorities, instead he was the one accused of Wrongdoing.)

Millions of men and women of all ages, ethnic, and racial backgrounds in this country (UK) hate going to work, gradually fall into despair and often become gravely ill. Some flee from jobs they used to love; others endure the situation unable to figure a way out. "Every day is like going into battle. They never know when the next bomb would be dropped. They are afraid to trust anyone for fear of being betrayed by who-knows. Their physical and mental reserves are depleted. They search for relief the quickest way possible. What is going on? Why is this happening to me? What can be done? They ask questions but answers not forthcoming.

What we are describing here has been identified as **"mobbing" and "bullying" at the workplace.** Co-workers, superiors, or subordinates attack a person's dignity, integrity, and competence, repeatedly, over several weeks, months or even years. This person is subjected to emotional abuse, subtly or bluntly; frequent false accusations of wrongdoing, and is persistent humiliation.

Dr. Heinz Leymann, a psychologist and medical scientist, pioneered the research about this workplace issue in Sweden in the early 1980's. "He identified the behaviour as "mobbing" and described it as **"psychological** terror" involving hostile and unethical communication directed in a systematic way by one or a few individuals primarily against one individual." Lemann identified forty-five typical mobbing behaviours such as: withholding information, isolation, badmouthing, constant criticism, circulation of unfounded rumours, ridicule, yelling, and so on.

Because the Organization (Trust) ignores, condones, and even instigates the behaviour, it can be said that the victim is seemingly helpless against the powerful and numerous; and is indeed "mobbed." The result is always injury – physical distress, mental distress or illness, social misery. Frequently, but not always, there is resignation or expulsion from the workplace. Furthermore, sadly, the victims did not have a reputation of 1) NOT performing WELL; 2) not meeting Organisational Standards; 3) not getting along with others. Quite the contrary, often, those targeted had been esteemed members of the organization.

Although mobbing and bullying behaviours overlap, mobbing denotes a "ganging up" by the leader—organization, superiors, co-workers, or subordinates—who rally others into systematic and frequent "mob-like" behaviour. In contrast to bullying, mobbing (<u>AGM, Nurses and RO, RL</u>) is clearly a group behaviour. Bullying (AGM), on the other hand, denotes a one-on-one harassment. In a mobbing, management is often tacitly involved. Therefore, in such a case, a victim rarely can find recourse.

Mobbing can happen to anyone. **It is not aggression against someone who belongs to a protected class, i.e., discrimination based on age, colour, gender, race, creed, nationality, disability, or pregnancy.** For this reason, bullying/mobbing behaviours have been termed general or "status-blind" harassment by Prof. David Yamada of the Suffolk University Law School. **Sometimes it can be a combination as what happened to Dr Fair-Brain i.e., including Protected class Characteristics.**

Impact of Mobbing

Mobbing—the emotional abuse—is a form of violence. In fact, in the book Violence at Work, published by the International Labour Office (ILO) in 1998, mobbing and bullying are mentioned in the same list as homicide, rape, or robbery. Even though bullying and mobbing behaviours may seem "harmless," in contrast to rape or other manifestations of physical violence, the effects on the victim—especially if the mobbing is happening over an extended period of time—have been so devastating for individuals that some have contemplated suicide. For Dr Fair-Brain, though he was at Isle of Wight for two to three months, he had just come out of a stressful investigation at the Royal Derby Hospital where nurses bullied him during the Trust investigation. This was followed up by the stressful investigation by the GMC, which was partial, biased, and very unfair. As a result of my experience, I conclude that some cases of the "going postal syndrome" may have been a consequence of what those individuals perceived as emotional abuses on the job.

Mobbing and bullying primarily affect a person's emotional well-being and physical health. Depending on the severity, frequency, and duration of the occurrences, as well as the resilience an individual may have, many may suffer from a whole range of psychological and physical symptoms: from occasional sleep difficulties to nervous breakdowns, from irritability to depression, from difficulties to concentrate, to panic-attacks, hypertension, or heart attacks. What were occasional absences may become frequent and extended sick leaves. **Dr Fair-Brain experienced all the above except the Acute Myocardial Infarction**

(AMI) but was admitted to the A&E during the days of Trust Investigation with what mimicked AMI.

Many persons who have become a target of a mobbing are damaged to such an extent that they can no longer accomplish their tasks. In the end, they resign—voluntarily (which the doctor did) or involuntarily (terminated or forced into early retirement). Ironically, the victims are portrayed as the ones at fault, or the ones responsible their own downfall. And in numerous instances, the symptoms persist after a person has been terminated or has resigned; furthermore, the symptoms can continue, and intensify and can led to **the diagnosis of post-traumatic stress disorder (PTSD).**

Additionally, not only will a person's health and sense of well-being be seriously affected; their families and their organizations are gravely impacted as well. In fact, relationships suffer. **Dr Fair-Brain's wife developed a <u>Functional Neurological Disorder (FND)</u> which was quite distressful to both husband and patient herself.** Dr Fair-Brain was not allowed to work because of the GMC investigation so he had to be full time CARER for his wife who lost independent mobility. She has had multiple investigations and appointments that certainly needed a Carer. Most of the treatments and appointments are still on going, seven years after the doctor resigned his position.

How it Starts and Why It Happens

It often starts with a conflict, any type of conflict. However, no matter how hard an individual may try to resolve an issue, it does not get resolved. The individual apparently does not get recourse. The issue does not go away, and eventually escalates to a point of no return or of no resolution.

What could have been resolved with good will and the appropriate mechanisms in place, has now becomes a contest between who is right and who is wrong. Some of the accusations and demeaning attacks may be guided by a scapegoat mentality, the need for personal power over others, and by personal animosities, by fears or jealousies. In fact, the latter seemed to have been the source of the mobbing and bullying for Dr Fair-Brain. Instead, group-psychology and a complex array of social-organizational dynamics delay or de-rail conflict resolution.

How, you might ask, is this possible, especially since there seem to be more structures and laws designed to protect workers. How is this workplace behaviour—mobbing—so prevalent, and yet awareness about the issue so scarce? We believe there are three reasons.

Reason one: mobbing behaviours are ignored, tolerated, misinterpreted, or instigated by the company or the organization's management as a deliberate strategy. Reason two: this behaviour has not yet been identified as a workplace behaviour clearly different from sexual harassment or discrimination. Reason three: often, the victims are worn down. They feel exhausted, they feel incapable of defending themselves, and incapable of initiating legal action.

The Costs of Mobbing

In 1991, C. Brady Wilson, a clinical psychologist specializing in workplace trauma, wrote in the Personnel Journal (now Workforce Magazine) that real or perceived abuse of employees amounted to a loss of billions of pounds: "Workplace trauma, as psychologists refer to the condition caused by employee abuse, is emerging as a more crippling and devastating problem for employees and employers alike than all the other work-related stresses put together." The actual costs in terms of lost productivity, health care and legal costs, not to speak of the psycho-social implications, are yet to be measured.

Dr. Harvey Hornstein, professor of social-organizational psychology at Columbia University Teachers College, in his book Brutal Bosses and Their Prey, estimated that as many as 20 million Americans face workplace abuse on a daily basis—a near epidemic. Though not sure of the exact figures in the UK, it would not be considered speculation to estimate a large percentage, of workplace abuse, in this country.

Awareness Grows

Nevertheless, awareness is growing. Bullying and mobbing at work is increasingly discussed in the media and in professional organizations. Researchers in organizational behaviour are now devoting attention to this topic, and several articles have appeared in academic journals, additionally many books (devoted to work abuse, brutal bosses, bullying and mobbing) have been written over the last three years.

What Can Be Done?

Persons who have been mobbed or become targets of bullies have several options. Most importantly, they need to understand that there is a name for what they are experiencing, that the phenomenon is well known and is increasingly being researched in this country. They need to understand that they have become victimized, and that there is truly little that they could have done differently. Secondly, they need to evaluate all options–in the short-term, medium-term, and the long-term. In fact, evaluation of options should include asking questions: **1) Are there any untried recourses? 2) Is finding another job within the company a possibility? 3) Have preparations been made to get another job?**

4) What preparation is needed for the transition? 5) Is medical or therapeutic intervention necessary? Cautiously evaluate all options, be assertive and manage the situation carefully. We also advise victimized people to leave their workplace sooner rather than later; to accept temporary sacrifices instead of enduring ongoing humiliation; which could have much more serious health effects later. Dr Fair-Brain chose to leave the Trust, but even with that the CMO of the Trust tried to make it impossible for him to locate a working position anywhere in the country by writing **a very prohibitive Transfer Letter; and this was simply wickedness.**

Management too, needs to be vigilant and spot any early signs of mobbing. A company policy that enforces respectful treatment of employees, and rewards civility among employees, can avoid workplace mobbing.

Summary

Mobbing is emotional mistreatment, abuse, committed directly or indirectly by a group of co-workers directed at anybody. People who have been affected by mobbing have suffered immensely. Mobbing is as a serious workplace issue most often leading to voluntary or involuntary resignation or dismissal. The social and economic impact of the mobbing syndrome has yet to be measured in quantitative terms in workplaces.

Mobbing can only persist if it is allowed to persist. Organizational (NHS TRUST Authorities) leadership plays the most important part in its prevention. By enforcing decency, civility, high ethical standards in the workplace, and by creating a nourishing environment, bullying, and mobbing will not surface or survive. There are many enlightened managers and leaders, as well as many companies which are preventing mobbing. These serve as good examples and places of refuge. It is suspected the managers and leaders at the Isle of Wight were in the process of being enlightened.

Chapter # 7

EQUALITY, DIVERSITY, AND INCLUSION"

(A Mandatory Training Module; NHS)

Abuse: What is Abuse? Where does it occur? Why does it occur?

Abuse occurs in schools, recreation, sports areas, and places of work. An Organisation must have a Zero-tolerance to Abuse. The Organisation must adopt and implement a policy of best practice and ensure procedures are in place to deal with abuse at a Workplace. Was the Isle of Wight NHS TRUST aware of these stipulations?

"You should never use profane, insulting, harassing or otherwise offensive language". However, the Isle of Wight NHS TRUST allowed T R, an A&E Consultant to use profanity, at will, against another medical colleague and the TRUST either condoned or was complaisant about the profanity.

Dr Fair-Brain cared very much about it because he detests profanity.

"You should never allow allegations of abuse or poor practice to go unrecorded" but when Dr Fair-Brain complained about abuse to his Supervising Manager it was totally ignored.

Dr Fair-brain was looking for someone who could help him against the emotional bullying and harassment he was suffering but he could not find anyone. He was left alone to face baseless and senseless allegations. **He was betrayed by and failed by the System.**

What did Dr Fair-Brain really suffer?

Dr Fair-Brain suffered the "actual severe adverse effects on the emotional and behavioural development caused by the persistent or severe emotional ill-treatment" and NO appropriate action was ever taken by the Trust despite the complaints. Dr Fair-Brain was exposed to a hurtful and discriminatory environment both deliberately and inadvertently. He had gotten into a state of mistrust; he did not know whom to trust or to whom to turn. M N and DA had a meeting with Dr Fair-Brain where he mentioned the bullying and harassment. DA encouraged the doctor to record future acts of bullying and harassment that he observed, and action would be taken, but instead action was taken against <u>HIM</u> because when the "**Group of Four**" heard about the report to the General Manager and his Supervisor, **they decided to do everything possible they could conjure to destroy and derail Dr Fair-Brain before anything turned against them.**

There was No Equality at St. Mary's Hospital – people were NOT treated regardless of colour, creed or ethnic background. As we know, Equality is not about favouring the minority group, it is about treating **everyone** regardless of any visible or invisible factors such as a person's gender, sex, colour, ethnic origin, faith, or religious beliefs (protected characteristics). Equality of opportunity is encompassed by legislation which makes treating someone unfairly not only immoral but also **unlawful.** Was the Isle of Wight NHS TRUST aware of this? What actually went on there? Who can ask the TRUST on behalf of Dr Fair-Brain and others who have experienced the same unfairness?

The definition of Discrimination is quite clear – treating individuals differently intentionally and unintentionally because of how they look (including colour of their skin), their beliefs of religious practices, gender, sexuality, lifestyle choice or preferences and physical or mental disability.

Dr TG Fair-Brain was a victim of deliberate hatred and discrimination which was seemingly condoned by the manager or even the supervisor and the TRUST and the GMC.

In brief, the doctor suffered all hatred, discrimination, emotional harassment, and victimisation. The harassment –unwanted conduct that violated his personal dignity or created an intimidating, hostile or offensive environment – was of great magnitude to the lonely doctor. The Victimisation – detrimental treatment–following the complaint he made because of the harassment and bullying was ignored by the TRUST. He was faced with both harassment and bullying – behaviour that was despicable, hurtful, intimidating, threatening, victimising, undermining, offensive, degrading, demeaning, and humiliating with no one to fight the injustice. When nothing is done by the TRUST or the Department of Health, who really listens? Who acts when a doctor is victimized? The same doctor was reported to the GMC worsening the situation instead of helping, the life of the doctor.

Bullying in a Workplace should be fought with every weapon at our disposal because it undermines the right to dignity of every well-meaning worker. How could the Isle of Wight be so complaisant by overlooking and violating human rights in such a manner? What really happens at this isolated health institution? It is filled mostly with locum medics because some practices are prohibitive at the place. It behoves the Department of Health to investigate.

During this period of investigation by the Trust, **Dr Fair-Brain was very Hurt and Stressed.** He was ANGRY by the lack of support, so much so, that his Blood Pressure became uncontrollably high. He had to be admitted into A&E for chest pains; he was prescribed some Anti-depressants and his colleagues from the Acute Oncology Service, involving the "Group of Four" did take the time to visit or to find out how he was doing. This was all happening within three to four months of being at the Trust. It appears to have been strong feelings of distaste for the doctor by the Trust as a whole. The most unfriendly four included the White chemotherapy sister, the **Clinical Nurse Specialist, the Assistant General Manager of the Acute Oncology Services, and the A&E Consultant.** The others who were attempting to derail the doctor:

Assistant Clinical Lead, Chief Med Officer, HR Officer and the Investigator, Dr M and The Appraiser. Dr Fair-Brain was put through Hell, by these people who did not care who they destroyed or killed with their false allegations. The SYSTEM supported the perpetrators – because <u>White</u> is <u>Right</u>, if you are <u>Black,</u> you <u>Lack</u> and must stay <u>Back</u>. NOTHING the doctor said was respected or considered to be TRUE. Was this another Black issue of Racism which is still common on God's planet earth?

Dr Fair-Brain decided the best thing to do was to leave the Hospital because he was up against people who would never believe his truthful intentions. He applied for a similar position – Specialty Doctor at the Worcester Royal Hospital, and he was offered the position. However, when the Chief Medical Officer at St. Mary's Hospital heard about it, he sent a transfer letter that made sure Dr Fair-Brain would NEVER be offered the position. One of the consultants at the WRH place openly told Dr Fair-Brain that though they were impressed with him at the Interview, but the letter from the CMO at the IoW TRUST caused them to deny him the job. Additionally, this same letter would affect his employment anywhere in the country (UK). Indeed, he lost the position before he started. Why? What did Dr Fair-Brain do to cause such hatred towards him? Why did they hate him so much? He never did ALL the things they claimed he did. He meant well and not what was reported in the allegations.

The interesting thing was he was never warned about anything. One of the most important allegations was that his Clinical Practice was in question. They gathered eight patients who were examined by other doctors, and nothing wrong was confirmed to be as "the Group" had claimed. After that the allegations were changed to "He had an Attitude, and he was Guilty of Probity". Dr Fair-Brain was asking questions, but because of facial expressions of surprise he was accused of having a "Bad Attitude". For these False Allegations, the doctor was reported to the GMC. Somebody must have pretended to have knowledge "the Science of Affection".

Is this what the Commission of Care Standards, the Care Quality Commission, the GMC and the Department of Health Condone? Surely a TRUST's AIM cannot and should not be to destroy but to correct, to build and to improve a professional colleague for the good of the Trust and Health Care Team. But the IoW Trust's Aim was a blatant attempt to destroy this doctor's reputation once and for all. How could the Trust be allowed to make up stories to rid of a caring, committed, compassionate and competent professional just because he was of a different colour (Black) or different ethnic background? This was not only puzzling but Evil. Do we have any one in this great country who can put an end to such wizardry and hatred? Are we willing to allow such hateful individuals to destroy the lives and reputations of other people?

The position at the Trust in Oncology has been intermitted filled because the evil "Group of Four" remain in waiting, intending to analyse and to prey upon whomever they choose. They decide who comes or stays at the TRUST in the Acute Oncology Service. In the opinion of the author, a place which is led by wicked individuals who have no clue of where they are headed themselves.

Doctor T G Fair-Brain was lied to, dragged through false allegations by a bunch of hateful and wicked people because he happens to be one of those with "protected characteristics (Black and African ethnic origin)". We are living in a different age; let us clean up these archaic racist behaviours and feelings.

Chapter #8

THE GENERAL MEDICAL COUNCIL (GMC) CREATES 'CLIMATE OF FEAR'

The following, once again, is maltreatment directed mostly against doctors of colour or significant "protected characteristics". Racism and Hatred are very much alive in the United Kingdom.

The General Medical Council is creating 'a climate of fear' for doctors under investigation, fitness-to- practise proceedings, GPs have observed. Doctors demanded that GPs under investigation for alleged misdemeanours should be presumed innocent until proven otherwise.

They also called for the GMC to implement the recommendations of the independent report Doctors Who Commit

Suicide While under GMC Fitness-to-Practise Investigations, published in 2014.

This report found 114 doctors died between 2005 and 2013, while undergoing fitness-to-practise proceedings, including 24 suicides and four suspected suicides. Dr Fair-Brain refused to be pushed into self-mutilation and termination because God is much bigger than a small general medical council composed of selfish, wicked, and hateful bunch whose survival depends on the same Almighty, God. God, the Creator, is the One and ONLY who decides and determines his destiny. NOTHING happens without HIS permission.

Calling for the implementation of the nine recommendations by the GMC, Glasgow GP John Ip said the strain of investigations left doctors practising 'in fear for their registrations'. 'A change is needed, and it is needed now,' he said, speaking at the BMA LMCs (local medical committees) conference In London today.

"Sword of Damocles"

Hertfordshire GP KB-S said the often-lengthy investigation periods, sometimes taking two to four years, were 'hardly a reasonable time scale' to have the sword of Damocles hanging overhead. The GMC took from October 2014 to March 2018 "investigating" Dr Fair-Brain for fabricated allegations which were Racially Motivated and still ended up ERASING his name from the Medical Registry.

Swansea locum GP, EO told peers about the experience of a fellow doctor who had been investigated by the GMC. He said the doctor's patient had complained to the GMC because they would not prescribe diazepam — the reason being the GP had concerns that the patient was abusing the medication.

Dr EO said the GMC had sent out letters to around 10 practices this doctor had worked in and were asked if they had any concerns about the doctor. 'This doctor was hugely distressed,' said Dr EO. It appears that is the 'modus operandi' the GMC uses to harass and intimidate those they interrogate, something that is associated with medieval methods of investigating people.

'This is not good enough; we know the GMC has a responsibility to protect patients, but at the same time [it has] a responsibility to support and protect doctors". The behaviour of the GMC is both reprehensible and unacceptable. 'The current situation is archaic, unfair, hurtful, and needs immediate revision and correction.'

Traumatic experience:

Another doctor said: 'Being the subject of a patient complaint is one of the most traumatic events in a doctor's working life here in the United Kingdom especially if you are Black or Asian.'

The report recommendations include:

- Doctors under investigation should feel they are treated as 'innocent until proven guilty'. Dr Fair-Brain was treated like the worst enemy of the practice of medicine. Apparently, the GMC Investigating team knew what their aim was before they commenced their investigation.

- Reduce the number of health examiners' reports required for health assessments;

- Appoint a senior medical officer within the GMC to be responsible for overseeing health cases;

- Make emotional resilience training an integral part of the medical curriculum;

- Establish a National Support Service for doctors (who have not functioned effectively to the advantage of the GMC".

Any doctor who is being investigated by the GMC can access the Doctor Support Service, which the GMC has commissioned the BMA Doctors for Doctors unit to provide. The service provides (supposedly) free confidential emotional support from a specialty-trained fellow doctor accompanying a doctor to a hearing if their case has been referred to a Medical Practitioner Tribunal Service panel. (**Not Proved to be the Truth.**)

NHS Doctors 'face Discrimination'

Doctor T G Fair-Brain was lied to, dragged through false allegations by a bunch of hateful and wicked people because

he happened to be one of those with "protected character-istics (Black and African ethnic origin)". We are living in a different age; let us clean up these archaic racist behaviours and feelings.

Doctors working in the NHS face discrimination because of their race, gender, origin, and sexual orientation, according to a report. The British Medical Association (BMA) says doctors with disabilities also come up against barriers.

In many cases, they are discriminated against by other doctors working in the health service.

"The findings are published ahead of the BMA's annual repre-sentative meeting which starts on Monday".

The report is based on interviews with twenty-five doctors–six from ethnic minorities, four women, seven with disabilities and eight who are gay, lesbian, or bisexual.

Career obstacles

Most of the ethnic minority doctors all came from overseas. They said they had faced obstacles in their career. They cited a lack of information over how they could take up jobs in the UK and being passed over for jobs in favour of white candidates.

"Twice I was discriminated against 'white' candidates," said one unnamed doctor. "First was for a registrar job in a teaching hospital and then for senior registrar job in the 1990s." **One lady doctor friend of Dr Fair-Brain faced despicable** discrimination and hatred from the consultant in her Orthopaedic department and even the GMC because she was Black and from Africa and nothing else significant.

The women questioned said they often found it difficult to climb up the career ladder. Many said they were discriminated against because of their gender and skin colour. One unnamed female doctor said: "I had to work for one who I knew was completely opposed to women."

The doctors with disabilities had similar complaints. "If you have a weakness, you keep it hidden," said one doctor, who was not named.

"[You] would expect tolerance from doctors, but this is the worst group when dealing with their own," said another.

Others said they faced discrimination because of their sexual orientation. "My senior partner in the practice was very homophobic," said one. "Made jokes about homosexuals in front of me and made disparaging comments about gay patients."

'Uncomfortable reading'

The report calls for more to be done to tackle discrimination in the NHS.

Dr GR, chairman of the BMA's equal opportunities committee, said some of the findings made for difficult reading. "The doctors who participated in this study have told us that not enough is being done in the NHS to combat discrimination. It is most hurtful when this treatment results in termination of a young doctor's career because of Racism, discrimination, and hatred because of one's skin colour.

"The report makes uncomfortable reading–doctors are facing barriers to their career progression every day of their lives because of their race, colour, gender, ethnic background, disability or sexual orientation."

Dr R suggested it was up to doctors to try to change attitudes inside the NHS. "We are all responsible for creating the current environment and it is only through our collective and individual actions that we can start to move forward. This is not truly clear what the individual meant.

"Attitudes must change first and by launching this report the BMA hopes to spearhead this change. "The Department of Health said there was "no place" for discrimination in the NHS. But what has it done to make sure it does not exist any longer?

"The government is fully committed to diversity and equality of opportunity for all health service staff," said a spokeswoman. "There is no place for discrimination or harassment in the NHS on grounds of race or ethnicity, gender, sexual orientation, disability, religion, or age. The NHS workforce must reflect the population it serves."

Racism plagues the NHS, and it is getting worse.

It was published in current year that "racism plagues the National Health Service and it's getting worse". This appeared in an article in first quarter 2020.

A doctor of colour made headlines when a patient asked if he could have a white doctor instead of him. In a powerful interview, the doctor called our national health service a jewel in the crown, but one that needs to take appropriate action to stop the jewel from being tarnished. He is not alone in experiencing racism as a doctor. **Dr Fair-Brain experienced racism at the Royal Derby Hospital in 2013. The doctor's experiences reveal that the problem of racism in the health service is getting worse and supports the research results.**

The latest Workforce Race Equality Standard (WRES) report from NHS England showed that black and minority ethnic staff in the NHS are suffering from increasing levels of bullying, harassment, and abuse. Skip Ad Black, Asian and minority ethnicity (BAME) respondents reported worsening conditions since reporting began in 2016, when compared to their white counterparts. The number of BAME staff reporting bullying, harassment or abuse from patients, relatives, or the public rose from 29.1 percent in 2016 to 29.8 percent in 2019. For white staff, the number fell, from 28.1% in 2016 to 27.8% in 2019. When just considering that nearly a third of the NHS workforce has a black, Asian or minority ethnic background worker, one realises just how significant these figures are.

The findings are part of a worrying trend of inequality towards BAME doctors and NHS staff who are twice as likely to face disciplinary action. The findings of the report, so shocking bear repeating: the number of BAME staff reporting bullying, harassment or abuse from patients, relatives, or the public rose from 29.1 percent in 2016 to 29.8 percent in 2019. The percentage of BAME staff experiencing harassment, bullying or abuse from staff and colleagues in the last 12 months, has now a large increase — from 27 percent to 29 percent. The comparison with white colleagues, white staff members went from 24 percent to 24.2 percent. The number of BAME staff believing their Trust gives equal career progression and pro-motion opportunities fell from 73.4 percent to 69.9 percent. That gap grew from 14.9 to 16.4 percentage points. The share of BAME staff experiencing discrimination at work from a manager, team leader or other colleague climbed from 14 to 15.3 percent.

The racially unequal climate within the NHS is nothing new. A report conducted in 1993 found similar disturbing statis-tics. It is published, in the British Medical Journal (BMJ), that doctors with English names were twice as likely to move on to senior roles than those with ethnic names, despite having the same experience and training.

One doctor reports: **"Sadly the evidence on the ground is that ethnic minority staff face increased levels of bullying and harassment both as employees and caregivers. And they continue to face discrimination in terms of access to ser-vices and in career progression."** The doctor states also: 'This is important because there is such a shortage of doctors in the

NHS, and as the biggest employer of BAME staff, it needs to make sure that people are satisfied, or they won't choose to work in the NHS.' But, the doctor notes, the NHS has taken steps such as the WRES report, as well as its regular inspections into what happens to NHS staff within organisations. He continues: "This is all good but there is a long way to go before we can say that NHS staff can realise their potential in an organisation where the senior leaders and decision-makers are overwhelmingly white. What I'd to see happen is a greater focus by NHS management on tackling racial inequalities for both patient and staff. This is complex and difficult, but much can be done. It remains a fact that the metrics (for example access to services, bullying and harassment) for staff and patients has become worse (over the past 10 years). Admitting there is a problem is a good starting point, and then constant efforts for improving is critical. Otherwise, people will refuse to work in the system."

But 27 years after that report, the inequality is still being perpetuated against BAME doctors at the very beginning of their careers. Reports published last year showed that medical students who come from a minority background are less likely to get a job, with 75 percent of white applicants who sought speciality training posts being appointed compared to just 53 percent of their BAME counterparts. In an investigation published in February 2020, the British Medical Association and the BMJ found that medical schools in the UK are ill-prepared to deal with the racism and racial harassment experienced by ethnic minority students. Notably, last year, the Equality and Human Rights Commission reported UK universities recorded only five hundred sixty complaints of racial harassment over three and a half years, in contrast to 60,000 students saying they made complaints.

The issue of racism in medical schools is important because BAME students make up 40 percent of medical undergraduates, nearly double the 22 percent in universities generally. Melanin Medics, a group for African-Caribbean medicine students was set up to address the issue of racism and to prepare aspiring medics on what to expect. Founder OD said: "Racism in medicine is not a new problem and the lack of progress in sufficiently tackling racism and racial harassment means that the issue has not been prioritised as it should. It is rare to you speak to a medic from an ethnic minority background who has not experienced racism, whether it be in the form of microaggressions or overt racial harassment, such behaviour has come to be expected." DO thinks it is great that there more conversations about racism in the workplace, but it is just as important that these conversations lead to action. The doctor says: "The responsibility should not lie solely on the victim or a select few to address this behaviour but also on those around them to provide support by identifying and challenging this behaviour even when they themselves are unaffected."

The wicked clever ones know how to keep the complainants quiet; they will promise you the moon but do nothing. Dr Fair-Brain knows quite well that there is not much improvement, and doubts whether any effort, has been made. **The only reason for his unemployment, and erasure of his name from the medical registry was simply because his Skin colour is BLACK.** There was NO OTHER clear reason if one carefully examines his case.

We need more alliance in the NHS, and more definition of terminology in the state of Racism and BAME debate. Terminology matters when we talk about race. Indeed, the Black people and the brown people are tired of hearing 'you're dividing us' when talking about racism.

Read more: https://metro.co.uk/2020/03/10/racism-plagues-nhs-getting-worse-12294073/?ito=cbshare

Twitter: https://twitter.com/MetroUK | Facebook: https://www.facebook.com/MetroUK/

How can workplaces fight racism? What else can be done after hiring more Black and ethnic minority staff? A definition 'racial gaslighting' is needed, as well as an explanation of why is 'racial gaslighting" so damaging for people of colour? Additionally, women of colour, in medicine, must deal with sexism in addition to facing racism. Junior doctor NB tells us she was often mistaken for a nurse or asked when the doctor will be arriving. In her time as a medic, she and her peers have witnessed several racist incidents. She explains: "We had a patient who refused to see an 'Arabic' doctor. He said he'd been trained to shoot Muslims in Iraq. Another one of my friends, who is Pakistani, went to see a patient as a medic; and was told her English was incredibly good. She was born in Surrey." What does the NHS have to say about these examples of the racism and sexism women medics are facing? We asked the NHS opinions and thoughts about the WRES report which highlights the issue of racism. Professor SM, Deputy Medical Director for Education Reform, Health Education England tells us: "Health Education England is working with UK

partners, the GMC, and the Royal Colleges to better understand the factors relating to differential attainment experiences
for all ethnic minorities and women. Furthermore, it com-
missions research, ensures recruiters have up-to-date training,
employs a robust complaints and appeals process, delivers best
practice guides and has established the Widening Access to
Specialty Programme (WAST) in order to give international
medical graduates experience in the NHS and to support their
applications into specialty training programmes." Sadly, and
unfortunately, the problem of racism in the NHS not only
affects staff members but also perpetuates the Prejudices and
biases held by doctors, affecting their patients as well. SS a
forty-nine-year-old black woman, contacted us to say she
has endured racism at the hands of doctors for the past three
decades. She says it is ironic that the NHS is discriminatory
towards black people since "the NHS was saved and propped
up by Caribbean nurses of which my mother was one" she
said. She had one personally harrowing incident. She had an
appointment for an abortion, but instead she was 'slut-shamed'
and given false information. She thinks she was "slut-shamed"
because of the doctor's personal prejudice. The doctor said,
"There is a six-month waiting list, and so I cannot not help you."
She continued, "I had done my research; I investigated all my
options, and obviously abortions have to be carried out within
a certain amount of time. There was no six-month waiting list
basically and he thought I was stupid enough to believe that." I
cried my heart out all the way home on the bus, from the shame
and humiliation I felt; it was excruciating. I was already embarrassed prior to attending the hospital appointment. Having to
go private, at a cost of £300, really affected my family. My father
was retired, and my mother had a part-time income. There was

not enough time to restart the process on the NHS, therefore I had to go private. We struggled with paying bills and buying food for months, which caused tension and arguments in our household. The incident was thirty years ago, and yes the doctor thinks the racism has continued from then to now.

We have also received multiple stories about racism in the NHS and other institutions that have a similar problem. It is important for the organisations to recognise the problem, to hold themselves accountable and to take adequate action. In order to understand the true extent of the problem, data must also be accessible – notably, Dr E was threatened with legal action by medical schools when he asked about obtaining figures for his report. Universities and medical schools should be transparent about the realities of their institutions and take necessary action to call out racism in a quick and efficient manner. After all, the NHS has been propped up by people of colour.

Read more: https://metro.co.uk/2020/03/10/racism-plagues-nhs-getting-worse-12294073/?ito=cbshare

Twitter: https://twitter.com/MetroUK | Facebook: https://www.facebook.com/MetroUK/

A Candid Statement about the GMC, UK (borrowed)

The General Medical Council, which is supposed to spend its huge income preserving medical standards, should have realised the effect that reduced working weeks would have on patient care. However, the GMC, which was once a rather lumbering but reasonably reliable organisation run by the medical profession to maintain a register of all doctors, and to mete out punishments to the bad ones, instead has become a political nuisance. It is, it seems to us all, of no practical value to patients or doctors but of enormous practical value to politicians and bureaucrats. The GMC's main role today seems to be to create ever more complex rules and regulations to keep its bureaucrats busy; and to justify its vast overheads. ("Like many quangos and quango-like organisations the GMC also likes raising money. Money needed to pay the vast salaries of all the administrators it has acquired. Many of whom exist to help GMC raise more money. There are licence fees and registration fees and there will soon be revalidation fees and fees for doctors who want to go to 'take a lick'".)

Thank God for the Brexit. The bottom line is that the GMC is a multi-million-pound money making machine with plush offices in central London. And that is about it. I believe it is self-serving and is far too pro-establishment. Considering 'all the good it does for patients and doctors' (it could be replaced by a single clerk equipped with a computer and a website). The GMC is a rich and hugely successful licensing body, which seems to us, to exist for the express purpose of collecting money rather than for protecting patients or defending the interests of doctors or improving medical standards. It is not only out of touch with reality, but also completely fails to understand the extent of the iatrogenesis of problems of racism.

Inquiries into the medical practices of ethnic minorities are not a matter of public record. However, the GMC will publicly denounce and pronounce judgement if a doctor found guilty of kissing, groping, or propositioning a willing patient; or helping a patient with their spiritual portion of their lives that relate to medical practice. After all, it is reasonable that if you are investigating the cause of an ailment, the spiritual state of the patient is an option a doctor can choose in taking a complete history of the patient. That is being thorough Apparently, spiritual life or lack thereof is something foreign to most. Especially of those unbelievers sitting behind their <u>big desks</u>, in the plush offices pretending to be doing something. Yet another form of discrimination, faith-based discrimination. On the other hand, doctors can put patients in danger medically, with no repercussions if the basis of decisions are racially and religiously motivated. On the other hand, a racial minority or religious minority is investigated and punished for the mere opinion of peers and investigators. There are two standards of judgement: the killing patients is fine, except of the doctor killing patients is **<u>a person of colour (BLACK).</u>**

The GMC launches investigations, and then makes biased judgements. These biased judgements are chiselled in stone. It is absurd (and, surely, questionably legal) to have a single body launching an investigation and then making an arbitrary judgement that will affect the lives of the doctor and his family. Patients and doctors deserve (and need) much more than an organisation which, like so many quangos, now seems to exist only to exist, and in practice, a support agency for the unholy trinity of State, drug industry and medical establishment.

Today, the General Medical Council of the United Kingdom gives a false sense of security and leadership. It is far worse than useless. I believe that without it, many of the problems we have today would have been tackled and made right by a more efficient organisation. The General Medical Council of the United Kingdom gets rid of committed, caring, compassionate and competent doctors of colour (especially Black) while pretending to be such "a competent watchdog" for the practice of medicine in the country. Who are they fooling really?

Chapter #9

THE DEVIL IS TRULY EVIL {GENESIS 50:20, ISAIAH 54:13-17}

Located at the lower most portion of Great Britain is an island called the Isle of Wight. Many people are excited to escape to the island for a week's break away from the hustle and bustle of mainland England.

I, T Gordon Fair-Brain, had the most awesome opportunity of not only visiting this beautiful island, but also was able to obtain employment there as a Specialist Doctor in Medical Oncology. This excitement was temporary, and suddenly turned into a nightmare! A nightmarish experience filled with emotional entrapment and trauma–after only two months of employment at the infamous Trust.

After I was invited for interview for the position of Specialist Doctor in Medical Oncology; I was thrilled to hear I had been offered the position. The hour-long boat ride from the mainland England to the hospital was both exhilarating and amusing. Little did I know the Isle of Wight was soon to be the camp of the most heinous demons. My excitement soon turned into a tormenting experience of "Racism, Hatred and Hurt". I will never forget my experience on this island as long as I live. The devil showed me what he could do to disrupt a child of God's dreams and destiny. More importantly, God showed me who He truly was, and what He desired for His creation. I discovered that I was NOT in control but that He was in control. and that He has always been in control. He knew from where I came, and to where I was going, and how I was going to get there. He was the Special Pilot, and I was His passenger.

They say anticipation fuels imagination. I was desperate to settle in on the Isle of Wight, and to commence my duties as a Specialty Doctor at the Trust in the department of Acute Oncology Services. There was nothing intimidating about the position, because I had worked in a bigger department in the same capacity before. I would be able to handle this new assignment with no problems. I anticipated the most glorious time of my life on the island. It felt as if I was on an extended holiday. I repeat, so that it is clear to you; coming over by boat it was as if I were going on a summer holiday.

To whet my appetite, I noticed roaming gangs of sea gulls, angry birds strutting their stuff, head down, beady-eyed marauders dashing to and from in their eternal fuss. I dreamt of standing at the seashores. I breathed deeply, a sigh of relief! I have arrived. I thought waters would be turquoise in colour gently warm to the toes, the diffused sun rippling with the rhythm and power of the waves subdued in gentle lapping. I could experience all of this from a house I had started renting in Shanklin. My daydreams of a summer holiday, now replaced by suffocating anxiety I felt as I awaited the chance to register as one of the islanders.

As I already stated, the moments of excitement on the island were turned into moments of regret and of being "time trapped". The sun still shone, while the emotional clouds of impending doom began rolling rapidly in the sky. The familiar landscape I had enjoyed, the coffee shops and poolside chairs all seem to lose their warm invitation after the sudden change at the Trust. Truth be told, the hospital hallways seemed to be teeming with 'spiritual hitmen', aka demons stalking me. Truth be told here; I could not see the demons stalking me. It was the fearful apprehension in me as I began this new adventure, on the Isle of Wight. As usual, I read from the Healing Word to receive the guiding and comforting Word from my Father, GOD. I knew God was bigger than the little demons hiding along the corridors of the hospital. "Greater is He that is in me…"

"I spent sleepless nights praying, meditating, crying, wondering and thinking what was going on."

The sweet and kind people – doctors from the mainland, nurses, and other colleagues – changed for the worse. There was a presence of intimidation. It appeared that even the walls were screaming "**you don't belong here…**" I refused to be intimidated but it was not until the **Chief of All Demons** instructed **the two demon-possessed nurses to commence my derailment.** It was easy for them because we shared an office, yet I had no idea of the evil plan they were up to. Finally, I was betrayed with False Allegations which the White Disciplinary Panel swallowed like a thirsty camel for water. The allegations against me were upheld and I was given a year's Warning. One would have thought that was enough and would have thought it ended there; but more instructions from the **Enemy, the Accuser of the brethren, Satan himself, intended to have his practice and life destroyed once and for all. But did he? The Panel reported him to the wicked, racial, and ruthless General Medical Council of the United Kingdom with NO clear or reasonable allegations.**

In his previous communications, he stated that a doctor under GMC investigation, whether for legitimate reasons or not, does not receive much support from the latter. Instead, the GMC appears to be at the forefront of lashing out harsh, hostile, and cruel treatment to the doctor. **"Doctors" are deemed guilty before trial and treated very mercilessly and without respect. No one cares whether they survive or not during the period of this unfair investigation especially the doctors of Colour (BLACK and BROWN).**

I hate you "Niggers". You are Black and Lack; stay Back until you Crack.

The doctor has suffered mercilessly during the so-called investigation period by the General Medical Council over the past four plus years. He was NOT interrogated by anyone from the GMC during the Investigation, and not that he was so eager for it; but he would have been pleased to have told the GMC the TRUTH of what transpired at the Trust. There were some truths GMC did NOT know. But did they care for the Truth? No! They did not. (Racism in the office: he was tested as if a thief, betrayed in day light – the Hospital and the GMC did not care at ALL. The lack of care hurt him. It was the possible source of the Racial Hatred that led to the false allegations.

It also became evident to the doctor that the GMC took long to investigate him, because there were no significant charges, or accusations. It appeared the time was used to search for minor errors they could place their fingers on within the two months of the doctor being at this Trust. There was not much evidence against him in two months, so they reached out to other the institutions where he had been. That was the plan, to find something substantial to stick on him and to destroy the doctor. They had made up their minds regarding what their decision with the IMG doctor, of colour and African origin, even before detailed investigation was carried out.

The doctor, however, stated that he had been denied years of work or being involved in the career he so dearly loved. He was not allowed to work because of these False and Racial Allegations. He loved working as a medical doctor for the people, God's Creation. He had worked or served patients with Love, Care, Commitment, Competence and Compassion, despite what the hateful demonic spirits stated or might have preferred to say and despite what they wanted everybody to believe. All the accusations were from the pit of hell.

The Suspension, he received, lasted many months; because, as per GMC Lawyer, he was "a risk to patients and the public ..." (but was NOT a risk when he worked from **September 2000 to June 2016**). And he never lost a patient for 15 years that he worked in the UK before he was accosted by the emissaries of Satan.

The GMC had been looking for the smallest infraction of the restrictions imposed on the doctor so they could jump up and say, "here is the evidence ... the doctor is stubborn and a serious risk to patients or public". Be warned, diabolical emissaries are still well and alive in the offices of the General Medical Council. Most of those working there were heartless and did not care whose life they destroyed especially if they were dealing with non-Caucasians. It takes spiritual eyesight to see the adversary; you cannot see him with the naked eye, and you cannot comprehend how evil the devil really is.

The doctor could not explain to anyone the state he was driven into by the investigation of the ruthless and hateful GMC officials. He cried until he could cry no more; he became anxious and fearful until he developed a fearless attitude, and he was stripped of the meagre savings he had. He rapidly went downhill financially. He borrowed money from friends, banks, and people he would never think of borrowing from. He fell into a financial CRISIS which he, on his own, could have never come out of. He became like a man without a name or surname, without respect, dignity, integrity, character, with no friend and no one to bless and encourage me. Even the pastor at his local church that he attended social-distanced himself from him though it was not time of COVID-19. He disliked me for reasons he could not explain. He was more than a laughing stalk. But he, however, refused to allow circumstances to eclipse his Godly Calling and to dictate his identity. He refused to allow the enemy to short-circuit his connection with his Father, God. He focussed his eyes on his wind shield and not on the rear-view mirror.

The Invisible Face is watching closely

He never lost one patient of the fifteen years he had worked in the United Kingdom as a doctor. He cared so much for human life.

Why such hatred from everyone? God, help me," He lamented.

Presently, he has a patient who happens to be his wife, she was treated like rubbish by one consultant at the Norfolk Norwich University Hospitals. He would have never treated any patient like that. On a second visit, he went with his wife and this time the Locum Consultant was a Saint because he heard the husband (a doctor) was present. It appears these are the doctors favoured by the GMC; he was not black. He will not go further into the distresses and the insults the favoured doctor, caused his wife; maybe this is what is condoned by the GMC. But as for him he did NOT believe in "snitching on other colleagues. He lets his Father, God, to be the Judge and Jury of such behaviour.

After his wife was seen by the neurologist and neurosurgeons, she still could not walk normally; she is still dragging her left leg, experiencing pins and needles with numbness in the whole left leg. She still has problem with urinary and bowel incontinence and weakness of the left arm with moderate to severe pain in the lower back. **All this was associated with the emotional pain and suffering she saw her husband go through, hence the non-specific diagnosis she was given.**

Diagnosis: The Experts could NOT place their fingers on the aetiology. It was a spiritual illness orchestrated by Satan himself such as the attack the doctor experienced while at the Isle of Wight. Finally, she was told she had **Functional Neurological Disorder (FND)**, a typical diagnosis of **"Not sure of the cause"**. She has had to stay on a pharmacy of drugs to relieve the neuropathic pain. They both knew, however, that she would be healed in time, Yes, I said, healed not just cured.

He was invited to Manchester for the Hearing on 17 March 2017. He genuinely wanted to go; hoping that he would have been granted a warning for whatever he did and then, permitted to return to work as a doctor but considering that the GMC cares so much for the welfare of patients, it would have been gross negligence of Dr Fair-Brain to leave his wife (a patient) at home alone, so he did not travel to Manchester. He had been her CARER since October 2016 being paid £62.70 per week (used to be paid £65-£70 per hour as locum doctor). But would you believe the same GMC thought he should have attended the Hearing in Manchester and leave the patient alone. The patient who was also his wife. It appears one cannot win for losing when dealing with this Council especially for those of us with "**protected characteristics**".

He was trying to leave no room of criticism by anyone including the GMC, so he felt it wise to demonstrate that patient's welfare comes first. If he left her alone and something happened, he would have certainly been considered a "'risk' to patients and the public". It so happened, he was also financially embarrassed; and the trip to Manchester was not feasible for him at the time. He had not been anywhere near a hospital, so he did not have much to contribute to the meeting and most importantly he had not violated any of the restrictions, but "**Mtetwa**" **did not sound like a Caucasian name, so it was easy to decide against the doctor.** Many doctors with genuine infractions on 'Good Medical Practice' are working today because **they were White and had legal support which Dr Fair-Brain could not afford.**

During this time of testing, the doctor's faith was tested to the limit, but he refused to turn his back on his God, Jehovah. Although he suffered, and at times was so discouraged that he despaired of his life, his Faith in God was unshakable and could not be destroyed, instead this increased his faith, and he has remained true to God. Dr Fair-Brain said, "Though He slays me, yet will I trust in Him" (Job 13:15). The doctor had confidence that God's eyes were upon him and that He would be victorious. Almighty God would show him favour and take him through the harsh times of testing. Dr Fair-Brain said, "But He knows the way that I take: when he has tried me, I shall come forth as gold". He knew God was in control of his life and circumstances, and that Nothing could come between him and his GOD. Like Job, "He came to understand that there was a spiritual reason behind his trial, suffering and even sickness". <u>God is greater than GMC, MPTS, and ALL the racists in this world.</u> He is greater than the pain, the financial crisis and the emotional problems he faced along the way. He have declared, "For I know my redeemer lives and HE shall..." see me through it all. His Word says, from Isaiah 43:1-2 "... Fear not, for I have redeemed you; I have called you by name, you are mine. When you pass through the waters, I will be with you; and through the rivers they shall not overwhelm you; when you walk through fire you shall not be burned, and the flame shall not consume you (my son)." We Win because "...those with us are more and mightier than those we see".

Isaiah 54:4: "Do not fear, for you will not be ashamed; Neither be disgraced, for you will not be put to shame; for you will forget the shame of your youth and will not remember the reproach of your (aloneness) widowhood anymore." (54: 4, 14-15 and 17).

Psalms 91: 7-8 A thousand may fall at your side, ten thousand at your right hand, but it will not come near you. You will only look with your eyes and see the recompense of the wicked.

Psalm 91:9-13 "Because you have made the Lord your dwelling place—the Most High, who is my refuge—No evil shall be allowed to befall you, no plague (even the Corona virus) come near your tent. For he will command his angels concerning you to guard you in all your ways. On their hands they will bear you up, lest you strike your foot against a stone. You will tread on the lion and the adder; the young lion and the serpent you will trample underfoot."

Chapter # 10

IS HATRED THE ROOT CAUSE OF RACISM?

Fear is the root cause of racism. People are inherently scared of what they do not understand. And sometimes when you do not understand something enough, and it scares you, you either hate it with all your guts, or you run away from it.

'Face of extreme Hatred for Race and Colour'

Was Hitler a racist regarding black people? Yes, he was!

Hitler regarded "Negro blood" in Europe as a contamination of the White race. Some of the French occupational troops in Germany after WWI were African. Hitler believed that both the Jews and the French deliberately put them in Germany to lower the political and cultural level of the Germans via race-mixing. Notice: Other races lowered the political and cultural level of the Germans. This implied that mixing with Blacks did not just make the mixed-race offspring impure, but also lowered the intelligence of its European parent. A large portion of the mixed-race children of Afro-French troops and German...belief was:

Racism is the belief that humanity is split into races with some races being superior to others.

Even before World War II, Germany struggled with the idea of African mixed race German citizens. While interracial marriage was legal under German law at the time, beginning in 1890, some colonial officials started refusing to register them, using eugenics arguments about the inferiority of mixed-race children to support their decision. By 1912, this had become official policy in many German colonies, and **a debate in the Reichstag over the legality of the interracial marriage bans ensued.** A major concern brought up in debate was that mixed-race children born in such marriages would have German citizenship and could therefore return to Germany with the same rights to vote, serve in the military, and could also hold public office as full-blooded ethnic Germans.

After World War I, French occupation forces in the Rhineland included African colonial troops, some of whom fathered children with German women. Newspaper campaigns against the use of these troops focused on these children, dubbed **"Rhineland bastards", often with lurid stories of uncivilized African soldiers raping innocent German women, the so-called "Black Horror on the Rhine".**

Young Rhinelander who was classified as a 'bastard' and hereditarily unfit under the Nazi regime.

Rhineland Bastard (German: _Rheinlandbastard_) was a derogatory term used in Nazi Germany to describe Afro-Germans, believed fathered by French Army personnel of African descent who were stationed in the Rhineland during its occupation by France after World War I. There is evidence that other Afro-Germans, born from unions between German

men and African women in former German colonies in Africa, were also referred to as *'Rheinlandbastarde'*.

After 1933, under racist Nazi policies, Afro-Germans deemed to be *'Rheinlandbastarde'* were persecuted. They were rounded up in a campaign of compulsory sterilization.

In the Rhineland itself, local opinion of the troops was quite different, and the soldiers were described as "courteous and often popular", possibly because French colonial soldiers harboured less ill-will towards Germans than war-weary ethnic French occupiers. While subsequent discussions of Afro-German children revolved around these "Rhineland Bastards", in fact, only 400–600 children were born to such unions, compared to a total black population of 20,000–25,000 in Germany at the time.

In *Mein Kompf*, Hitler described children resulting from marriages to African occupation soldiers as **a contamination of the white race:** "by Negro blood on the Rhine in the heart of Europe." He thought that "Jews were responsible for bringing Negroes into the Rhineland, with the ultimate idea of bastardizing the white race which they hate and thus lowering its cultural and political level so that the Jew might dominate." He also implied that this was a plot on the part of the French, since the population of France was being increasingly 'negrified'.

Rhineland sterilization program

By that definition Hitler clearly stated what he thought in
<u>Mein Kampf</u> in which he believes Africans are inferior com-
pared to Aryans. That was racism.

Also, we can ask an Afro-German who actually had to live in
Nazi Germany:

This is a story of the unexpected. In Destined to Witness, Hans
Massaquoi has crafted a beautifully rendered memoir — an
astonishing true tale of how he came of age as a black child in
Nazi Germany. The son of a prominent African and a German
nurse, Hans remained behind with his mother when Hitler
came to power, due to concerns about his fragile health, after
his father returned to Liberia. Like other German boys, Hans
went to school; like other German boys, he swiftly fell under
the Fuhrer's spell. So, he was crushed to learn that, as a black
child, he was ineligible for the Hitler Youth. His path to a
secondary education and an eventual profession was blocked.
He now lived in fear that, at any moment, he might hear the
Gestapo banging on the door — or Allied bombs falling on
his home. Ironic, moving, and deeply human, Massaquoi's
account of this lonely struggle for survival brims with courage
and intelligence.

Pandemic Racism for generations

Humans, by nature, are fickle beings. The government of the UK originally joined the EU. Membership made travel and trade easier. Then Brexit happened. Now free trade and travel are removed. Many older British were for Brexit because they feared the influx of foreigners especially from Europe because they would …? Whether the blame is fear of foreign values, tradition, or demographics of our societies this has been unclear. Change is hard for many, so it seems that xenophobia became the root cause of Brexit.

People became scared of different races, they did not know what to expect from them, but they *knew* that these people are different. These people look different, eat and dress differently, worship differently and possible work differently. On the other hand, knowing that people are different also makes it easy to blame bad things on the foreigners because of distrust for them. This has been repeated in history, whether it was with Jews, or Blacks, it's a reoccurring theme.

We human beings can either assert dominance or be dominated. Assertion of dominance is the trait I see in racists. However, after generations of dealing with different races, and building our own conscience, there is still in some people, a second-hand fear, and this becomes an irrational hatred.

Even today, we have things like "intellectual racists" who try to back up their bigotry with statistics, and with public policy.

At the end of the day, they are still scared, that perhaps that there is not an inherent genetic difference, but a social one. It is easier to blame things on people if you believe that it is their inherent nature. Many white people believe it is the inherent nature of black people to be thieves and be untrustworthy. It is much harder to fix something when you recognize it is a structural versus cosmetic or societal versus individual. Honestly speaking, let us face it, some people just do not want to own responsibility for ignorance, fear, and hate.

A rational belief and rational narrative will be replaced with an irrational belief system and irrational narrative, for example:

1) "They're stealing our jobs, keep them out!"

No, not everyone saying this is necessarily racist, but there is a token many who use this as *a* cop out to show dislike for people that do not look like them.

2) "He was asking for directions, but he might have tried robbing me. I had to shoot him. He looked scary."

3) "Keep these 'Black' people out of our communities. They're all thieves and cannot be trusted." I used to hear a lot of this when I first arrived in the United States of America.

4) "Look at them! They are just coming here to take over our civilized and peaceful communities and destroy the social framework. You can't trust them."

5) "Oh? Do all five of those kids really have the same father? That's rare of these black people."

6) "Speak English! Keep your language out of here!"

These are all Racist thoughts. Parroting a token few words is easier than thinking for yourself. Everyone wants to think they are rational, but emotions hinder rational thoughts for many.

Truth be told, sometimes, people just genuinely do not care. If racism is easy for them, they will take the easy way out. To me, the root cause of racism is fear. Racists, and bigots of any breed, are just scared of what is not them or is not theirs.

Biblical Solutions

Only Biblical Christianity offers a rational basis for opposing racism and for pursuing justice. Equality before the law is a Biblical principle: "The community is to have the same rules for you and for the alien living among you; this is a lasting ordinance for the generations to come. You and the alien shall be the same before the Lord. The same laws and regulations will apply both to you and to the alien living among you." (Numbers 15:15-16) But for many white Christians it is difficult to reconcile with such claims. **Christians I worshipped with in Ironton, Ohio, USA preferred that I went to churches where other Black people gathered. I did not understand what difference it made.**

Creation Leads to Respect for Life

If the Biblical doctrines of Creation and of Redemption (people are made in the image of God (Acts 17:26) are taught and heeded the causes and the effects of racism, affirmative action, xenophobia and hate speech; will be undermined. "Therefore, if anyone is in Christ, he is a new creation; the old has gone, the new has come! All this is from God who reconciled us to Himself through Christ and gave us the ministry of reconciliation: that God was reconciling the world to Himself in Christ, not counting men's sins against them. And He has committed to us the message of reconciliation." 2 Corinthians 5:17-19

Evolutionism Breeds Racism

On the other hand, those who hold to Darwin's theory of evolution, have no objective basis with which to counter racism. In fact, Darwinian evolutionism has inspired a whole host of racist ideologies and movements, especially communism. The actual title of Darwin's famous evolutionary book is: "On the Origin of Species by Means of Natural Selection, or the "Preservation of Favoured Races in the Struggle for Life."

Evolution Leads to Revolution

Karl Marx wanted to dedicate Das Kapital to Charles Darwin and wrote, "Darwin's book is very important and serves me as a basis in the natural sciences for the historical class struggle." "Violence is the midwife…" as Soviet dictator Joseph Stalin so succinctly put it, <u>"**Evolution leads to revolution!**"</u>

Darwin and Marx were Racists

Both Darwin and Marx expressed racist views. It is ironic that so many Russians and Africans have held Marxist and evolutionary beliefs because Darwin taught that the "**advanced races**" **should "exterminate" the primitive races to speed up evolutionary progress!** Would it surprise anyone to learn that there are many of the white people today who respect the Darwin/Marx views which explains why a **Black African Doctor finds himself suddenly surrounded by disciples of Darwin or Marx with positions in the GMC Offices.** They look at the Black African doctors trained at Cambridge Faculty of Medicine as a primitive despite their qualifications. Old white patients would rather have their consultation with a Caucasian doctor though the Black and Caucasian doctors were trained at the same College.

Karl Marx himself despised the Slaves and Blacks, writing that they were "frozen at pre-civilisation levels" and would never make any contribution to history! (Karl Marx – the

Racist, 1978; Understanding the Times, by David Noebel, 1991; Marx and Satan, by Richard Wurmbrand). Dr TG Fair-Brain was underrated as a professional from the time he arrived at the Isle of Wight (Hate & Hurt) as a nobody who could not contribute to the health and values of this Trust. He was asked how long he was going to stay at the hospital the second week of his work by the main Clinical Nurse Specialist (JB) who eventually betrayed him. It appeared she already had ideas of planning his derailment just as he started work there. "They promise them freedom, while they themselves are slaves of depravity..." 2 Peter 2:19

Discrimination and Antagonism

The Oxford English Dictionary defines racism as: "...discrimination against or antagonism towards other races." There was/is definite racism at the St Mary's Hospital NHS Trust unfortunately.

Hypocritical Racists

Yet many, who speak out against vitriolic behaviour (express bitterness and hatred) against racism, are themselves racist, displaying intense antagonism towards people of other races and advocating policies which discriminate on the basis of race. This sounds like some of the IoW Trust personnel and GMC Officers mentioned. Asked, they would swear by Gods created earth that they do not endorse racism. I could always tell racists from their quick confession of loving the black people even when they were not asked.

Character or Colour?

There are many white people who would have idolised Dr Martin Luther King (Jnr.), but who were not willing to live by his maxim that **people should be judged by the content of their character, not by the colour of their skin.** I certainly agree with the great orator. However, let me point out that it is the white individual who hides behind sheep's clothing; they hide their hate behind empty words. Judging by the colour of a person's skin. It seems the entire world certainly idolizes Dr Martin Luther King and his humanitarian contributions to mankind (especially for the black people). And of course, from **the continent of Africa was the statesmen Mr Madiba Nelson Mandela, who was adored by many across Africa, UK, and USA because he had selflessness and love for humanity.**

Murderous Manipulations

Frustrated people are easily manipulated by mesmerizing slogans sold by murderous hate-mongers. One of the easiest ideas to sell anyone is that he is better than someone else. History has done the white racist injustice because he has been told he is better than the man with black skin.

The holocaust in Rwanda where mobs of Hutus slaughtered over eight hundred thousand Tutsi Christians, is just one example of the destructive power of tribalism in Africa in recent years. More people were killed with machetes in six weeks in Rwanda, than have been killed by nuclear weapons in all of history.

In Zimbabwe the Ndebele people, the second largest tribe, were mowed down mercilessly by the ZANU-PF 5th Brigade and Satan is the only one who knew why. It is so easy to point at things happening many miles away, yet many black skinned people are gunned down every week by whites in the USA and young black men are carved with knives by white Skinheads in Britain. Black professionals are destroyed emotionally and intellectually by being removed from practising in their qualified professional roles such as medical doctors because of their Black skin in the NHS Hospitals in the United Kingdom and no one loses sleep over it. Nobody screams about this until it affects the so-called White people or if it has been so exposed by the media that it has resulted in a national outrage (Steven Lawrence case).

There is a pandemic evil and infectious spirit that has survived over 400 years which targets white people only and maybe some of those who believe they are white. The world, unfortunately, has not worked together collectively to come up with an effective vaccine that can wipe out <u>the Virus of Racism</u>. **An effective vaccine is needed urgently. It is believed a good vaccine usually takes years to develop; don't you believe it has been long enough.**

I asked God one time why a loving and caring God would allow suffering of some innocent people just because of their skin-colour. He didn't reply to me directly but assured me He controls all that was happening and that He sometimes lets **"US" be targets of "evil people "to alert us to the problem of sin, to direct us to respond to Him in faith and hope and that Nothing escapes His visual field. He is Omniscient.** Job was a vivid example of how a good person could suffer incredible tragedy because of Satanic attack permitted by God for His own glory. I cannot answer any other questions beyond this point. All I can say is God is a good God and He always knows what He is doing. He knows what lies beyond today.

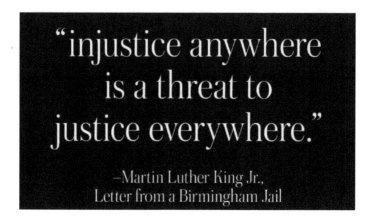

"injustice anywhere is a threat to justice everywhere."

–Martin Luther King Jr.,
Letter from a Birmingham Jail

Injustice and Racism are close allies

HATRED

Racism has been described as "the epitome of hatred for the smallest of reasons." That is a valid statement; the most insignificant reason led to the temptations, betrayal, and eventual destruction of one of the most caring, loving, and adored doctors by the hateful 'white' nurses with their accomplices all being Racially Motivated. Today the doctor is depending on benefits to survive. Are they pleased with this outcome? What have they gained? **"Preservation of the Favoured Races,"** Is that the aim? They are gluttonous for the suffering of other human beings and yet masquerade as philanthropists and compassionate Government officials protecting the public and patients and even promulgating their principles via 'democratic precepts'.

H.G. Wells noted that racism "justifies and holds together more baseness, cruelty and abomination than any other sort of terror in the world."

Double Standards

But of greatest concern are the enemy's weapons of **Hatred and Racism** today the world over; these cannot be attacked by physical weapons. Racism and Hatred can inhabit a nation and employment of the latest technology cannot rid of it. It is invisible, indestructible; it is sly and slippery and difficult to rid of. **Murambe** was an intelligent man but where did he learn his tactics? Who taught him to employ deluded diplomacy? The same 'white' people who are now crying "psychotic dictator".

The white people used to mow down hundreds of thousands of Africans to steal precious African minerals and there were no judicial courts to arrest and confine these wicked intruders. No one decried such actions. Today young, educated Africans still face despicable but subtle treatments in their home -United Kingdom–from the same 'white racists and killers'. Our 'black' colour is being used as a self-destructing weapon. They do not say, "You are black and so you are incapable and incompetent but, covertly say "**You are <u>black</u>, and you <u>lack</u> so stay <u>back</u>**" in the most inconspicuous way. "Whoever says to the guilty, you are innocent – peoples will curse them, and nations denounce them." Proverbs 24:24. "How long will the land lie parched and the grass in every field be withered? Because those who live in it are wicked, the animals and birds have perished."Jeremiah 12:4

Oppression

As a young man, Dr Fair-Brain grew around Racism in its true colour.

As a young innocent African growing up, **Gordon Fair-Brain was a victim of the South African Apartheid Policy and Racist Rhodesia.** He had nobody to whom he could report. Instead, he prayed to God to spare his life; for he would work hard and become somebody who can forgive and forget and train future young men and women (**Black and White**). He wanted to train others, regardless of colour to be caring, compassionate and loving individuals in their jobs and environments whether as professionals in medicine or other professions. Praying that, someday they would forget the hurtful and diabolical treatment handed down to them from history. **We did not have** to be like the White Racists of yester-year or psychotic Murambe's of recent history.

But what Fair-Brain faced when he completed his studies as a doctor in the United Kingdom in the 21st century was despicable and unacceptable. Though most of his white patients loved and adored him as a doctor, White nurses with their 'white accomplices' at **the Isle of "White" NHS Trust,** still devised a way of derailing an innocent black African professional by fabricating allegations which the "competent" General Medical Council swallowed without developing any allergic reaction, and of course colluded with the nurses in the derailment of this doctor's medical career. Although, he had never been fired, and the collusion against him worked. This doctor has never lost a patient, and he worked well with every clinical personnel in both Private and NHS hospitals of the United Kingdom. What a shame! What is the difference in the behaviour of the African psychopath in Zimbabwe who killed mercilessly and at random with **today's wicked and hateful Council which is guilty of collective insanity who will destroy doctor's lives because they are of a black skin, with impunity?** I thought the Council would try and support their doctors as much as possible until a doctor is found guilty of a serious and repeated misdemeanour, found to be a definite hazard to the patient and public with evidence beyond the shadow of doubt and not from circumstantial and biased evidence.

Dr Fair-Brain is not and has never been <u>a Paedophile doctor;</u> <u>a Harold Shipman</u> or a <u>Dr J Barton</u> who killed patients with purposeful overdosing with Narcotic drugs or <u>Mr S</u> <u>'Brumball', the proud surgeon, who was so good that he had</u>

tattooed his signature on patients' livers (11/01/2018 BBC News). these doctors only received slaps on their wrists from the GMC, and only acted when there was public outcry. On the other hand, **Dr Fair-Brain was ERASED immediately from the Medical Registry with NO hesitation.** The difference was that they were **"White"** and Doctor Fair-Brain was **"Black"** who had no clinical issues but **"had to be given a 'death' sentence with No Parole for stealing candy".** And you cry about the behaviour of the African dictator who was "practising in Africa what they preached" as they stole our beautiful and precious land which is blessed with rich minerals and precious metals. Today, much of the gold decorating the Royal Palace, here in the UK originated from my country of birth.

When colonialists usurped land from the black people in Africa

"Woe to those who call evil good and good evil, who put darkness for light and light for darkness... who are wise in their own eyes... who acquit the guilty for a bribe, but deny justice to the

innocent…they have rejected the Law of the Lord Almighty…"
Isaiah 5:20-24

Recognising Reality

We need to recognise that crime and violence; corruption and malice are symptoms of our society's rebellion against the Laws of God. "And have no fellowship with the unfruitful works of darkness, but rather expose them." Ephesians 5:11 Racism and hatred for people of colour is equally non-productive and contributes nothing to progress in our modern-day architecture.

The crime and violence are the symptoms of "**Hatred and Racism**", and they are very destructive forces whether in Africa, America, or United Kingdom. These destructive forces are evident in a few individuals: Hitler, Stalin, Murambe of Zimbabwe, and Idi Amin of Uganda. However, the destructive forces of hatred and racism can also be less evident, undetectable, and sly. It can hide behind the systems in hospitals, councils, organisations, and governments. Removing the demagogues and corrupt leaders (**Murambe, the Suma, Hitler, Stalin, Idi Amins**) **is not enough, hatred and racism need to be removed from the roots.** Removing one or two extremes from the Council is not enough, but extermination of the whole dysfunctional and inefficient fabric would be most beneficial. Similarly, cutting off tree branches of hatred and racism would leave the roots and tree trunks untouched; racism and hatred would continue to sprout, and people of certain class, colour, race, and origin will continue to suffer. God's created humanity will continue to suffer with no end.

Exposing Evil

The scourge of animism, tribalism, Islamic slave trade, genocidal clan warfare, the legacy of Nazi and Marxist hatred and Racism need to be exposed. "Who will rise for Me against the evildoers in Africa, Europe, America, United Kingdom, in the hospitals, business places in homes, in the streets etc? Who will stand up for me against the workers of iniquity?" Psalm 94:16 The Word of God says, **"Don't be afraid, for I am with you (Fair-Brain)! Do not be frightened, for I am your God! I will strengthen you- yes, I will uphold you with my saving right hand! Look, ALL who were angry at you will be ashamed and humiliated; your adversaries will be reduced to nothing and perish. When you will look for your opponents, you will not find them; your enemies will be reduced to absolutely nothing. For I am the Lord your God, the One who takes hold of your right hand, who says to you, 'Don't be afraid, I am helping you'..."** It is true, God Himself has been helping me since I was left stranded in the debris of confusion and filth; by those who created enmity with me.

Biblical Solutions

The Biblical solutions to racism, xenophobia and hate speech are found in the Doctrine of Creation, The Greatest Commandment (Love one another), The Golden Rule (Do unto others...), The Good Samaritan (serve your brother regardless of colour, race ...) and The Great Commission. How many people trust in God's Word, and how many will take counsel from this Great Book?

The Greatest Commandment

Our Lord Jesus Christ taught that the Greatest Command is: "Love the Lord your God with all your heart and with all your soul and with all your mind and with all your strength… Love your neighbour as yourself." Mark 12:30-31 Maybe this should be discussed and passed as law in the British Parliament, American Senate and Congress, European Institutions and African governments. This would be a step forward. Dr Fair-Brain tried to mention in one sentence that **God was The Healer, the Mysterium Tremendum, the Supreme Ruler, the Great Physician, and not a medic.** Afterward, he was reported to the wicked and ungodly authorities for inciting refusal of Chemotherapy. He believes that God is the Healer, yet his beliefs also contributed to the decision to terminate his License to practise medicine in the United Kingdom.

The Golden Rule

Our Lord Jesus Christ taught us to observe the Golden Rule: "And just as you want men to do to you, you also do to them likewise." Luke 6:31 The one that works the world over is 'Let me do to you what you do not do to me…'

Love Your Enemies

Jesus taught His followers to: "Love your enemies, do good to those who hate you, bless those who curse you and pray for those who spitefully use you…" (Luke 6:27-28) This does not work very well, and I do not believe many have tried it. I can forgive the people who aimed to destroy my career and life but loving them is another kettle of fish. I have to do it because I love humanity, God's creation.

The Great Commission

After rising from the dead, and before ascending into Heaven, the Lord Jesus Christ gave His followers the Great Commission: "All authority has been given to Me in Heaven and on Earth. Go therefore and make disciples of all the nations, baptizing them in the Name of the Father and of the Son and of the Holy Spirit, teaching them to observe all things that I have commanded you; and lo I am with you always, even to the end of the age." Matthew 28:18-20. Before you jump on to my throat, understand that I am merely sharing my beliefs with you; I am telling you is in the Bible. I respect your right to agree or disagree.

Christian Love in Action

Because of these and other Scriptural commands, Christians like St. Patrick, Boniface, William Wilberforce, John Newton, William Carey, David Livingstone, Mary Slessor, Lord Shaftsbury and General Charles Gordon, and many unnamed others, worked tirelessly to end the slave trade, stop child labour, and set the captives free. Amongst all the religions of the world, only Christianity brought an end to the slave trade. Dr G Fair-Brain is contributing all he has, to end hatred and racism; spiritual illness, emotional servitude as well as going through life on an empty tank hence this book.

Chapter #11

WHERE IS GOD IN THE STORM?

'When neither sun nor stars appeared for many
days and the storm continued raging, we finally
gave up all hope of being saved.' Acts 27:20 NIV

There are times when God seems inaccessible. When you
pray, you feel abandoned in your present circumstances.
And not just abandoned, but terrified and even hopeless. Paul
understood that feeling. He had longed for an opportunity to
preach in Rome and was on his way there when a hurricane
destroyed his ship. Paul not only foresaw the loss of the ship,
its crew and cargo, but 'our own lives also' (v. 10). He tried to
warn the captain of the crew about the impending tragedy, but
his words were disregarded.

In short, Paul and two hundred seventy-six others were placed
in a life-threatening position by the wilful disregard of others,
yet there was nothing he could do about it. Feeling a sense of
despair, he and his believing companions declared, 'We finally

gave up all hope of being saved!' Then after fourteen days lost at sea – when the hurricane was fiercest – God sent an angel. 'Do not be afraid, Paul…God has graciously given you the lives of all who sail with you' (v. 24) In other words, 'You will reach Rome, no worry'. **"This had to happen."**

When it looked like Paul's consuming desire to preach in Rome would be thwarted, God faithfully piloted them through the storm to the exact destination He'd planned for them.

"And we know that ALL things work together for good to them that love God, to those who are the called according to His purpose" (Romans 8:28). It so happened that after their ship was destroyed, they had reached an island called Malta. People there were quite hospitable. But why did God allow such a situation? We must learn and know; the grace of God does not spare you running aground. However, His grace will lead us to experience a place of refuge. It had to happen! Paul was at a small island, a place he had not planned to be. While they prepared a fire to warm themselves, Paul was bitten by a poisonous viper. Paul was able to shake it off; yet people expected to see him fall down dead. When he did not, they started thinking he was a god.

One preacher has said, we all need to go through "the University of Adversity". On Malta Paul was to experience yet another miracle. The father of Publius in charge of the island was sick with fever and dysentery. Paul was called in to help and he prayed over the man and was healed. When they finally left the island, they were sent off with plenty food rations for the rest of the trip. When I looked at my situation, I felt I should not have gone through all the hurts and suffering, but God had a reason for allowing me to go through it. There was a purpose for my going through it. "**It had to happen!**"

Paul would go to Rome and declare God's Word before Caesar. Life has its storms. Life has its trials. Whatever trial you (Gordon) are facing today, know this one thing: you can trust God to carry you through it NOT into it. He determines 'the end from the beginning' (Isaiah 46:10), so you will come out of this stronger and wiser.

What did Jesus mean when He said, "I am the good Shepherd?"

He said, "I am the good shepherd" (John 10:11) is the fourth of seven "I am" declarations of Jesus recorded only in John's Gospel. These "I am" proclamations point to His unique, divine identity and purpose. Immediately after declaring that He is "the door" in John 10:7, Jesus declares "I am the good shepherd." He describes Himself as not only "the shepherd" but the "good shepherd." What does this mean?

Jesus is "the good shepherd", not simply "a good shepherd", as others may be, but He is unique in character. The Greek word kalos, translated "good," describes that which is noble, wholesome, good, and beautiful, in contrast to that which is wicked, mean, foul, and unlovely. It signifies not only that which is good inwardly—character—but also that which is attractive outwardly. It is an innate goodness. Therefore, in using the phrase "the good shepherd," Jesus is introducing us to His inherent goodness, His righteousness, and His beauty.

As shepherd of the sheep, He is the one who protects, guides, and nurtures His flock.

As He did in declaring that He is "the door of the sheep" in John 10:7, Jesus is making a contrast between Himself and the religious leaders, the Pharisees. He compares them to a "hireling" or "hired hand" who does not really care about the sheep. In this narrative of the hireling and the hired hand I see similarities to the callous and ungodly people who work in the GMC, as those who do not care whom they destroy, especially if they are people of Colour. But the Creator, God does not miss all this unfairness and hatred which is known by the word Racism.

In John 10:9, Jesus speaks of thieves and robbers who sought to enter the sheepfold stealthily. In that passage the Jewish leaders (Pharisees) are contrasted with Christ, who is the Door. Here, in John 10:12, the hireling is contrasted with the true or faithful shepherd who willingly gives up his life for the sheep. He who is a "hireling" works for wages, which are his main consideration. His concern is not for the sheep (Godly, caring, and compassionate professionals) but for himself. Interestingly, the shepherds of ancient times were not usually the owners of the flock. Nonetheless, they were expected to exercise the same care and concern as if they were the owners. This was characteristic of a true shepherd. However, some of the hirelings thought nothing of the sheep. This is what we observe these days. The GMC of this country have heartless and diabolical hirelings. As a result of uncaring hirelings, when a wolf appeared—the most common threat to sheep in that day—the hireling abandoned the flock and fled, leaving the sheep to be scattered or killed (John 10:12–13).

In order to understand the purpose of a shepherd, during the times of Jesus. It is helpful to realize that sheep are utterly defenceless, and totally dependent upon the shepherd (good, caring and understanding). Sheep are always subject to danger and must always be under the watchful eye of the shepherd as they graze. In torrential rainstorms, walls of water rush into the valleys and may drown the sheep; unattended sheep may be stolen by robbers; and wolves may attack the vulnerable flock and kill.

In the Bible, during the war between the children of Israel and the Philistines, David tells the king of Israel how he killed a lion and a bear while defending his father's flock as a shepherd boy. Driving snow in winter, blinding dust, and burning sands in summer, long, lonely hours each day—all these the shepherd patiently endures for the welfare of the flock. In fact, shepherds themselves were frequently subjected to grave danger, requiring them to give their lives to protect the sheep.

Likewise, Jesus gave His life on the cross as "the Good Shepherd" for the world. He who had the power to save others, chose not to save Himself. "The Son of Man did not come to be served, but to serve, and to give His life a ransom for many". Through His willing sacrifice, and willing servitude the Lord made salvation possible for all who come to Him in faith on the other hand, Jesus spoke of the hireling: when danger is present, when the sheep needs protection; the hireling runs and saves his own life. The hireling does not care for the sheep and will not help. I compare my life in the UK to this parable. Because I am an African doctor, I am left to defend myself against enemy attacks. There is none who has lain down his life for me like the Good Shepherd, Jesus.

It had to happen. Jesus' death was divinely appointed. It is only through Him that we receive salvation. "I am the good shepherd; and I know My sheep and am known by My own". Furthermore, Jesus makes it clear that it wasn't just for the Jews (the Chosen people) that he laid down His life, but also for the "other sheep (non-Jewish Gentiles) I have which are not of this fold; them also I must bring, and they will hear My voice; and there will be one flock and one shepherd". The "other sheep" clearly refers to the Gentiles (all non-Jewish people including, black and Indians). As a result, Jesus is the Good Shepherd overall, both Jew and Gentile, who come to believe upon Him (John 3:16).

What is the valley of death?

Have you ever wondered what it is like in the "valley of death?" It does not sound like a fun place. . There is no such place as the valley of death. The phrase is a popularized misquotation of the Judeo-Christian Bible.

The original phrase is found in the Hebrew Scriptures, Psalm 23:4. From the King James, it reads:

"Yea, though I walk through the valley of the shadow of death, I will fear no evil: for thou art with me; thy rod and thy staff they comfort me."

The original phrase in its entirety is the "valley of the shadow of death." The difference is subtle, but important. The shadow of death implies a situation where death looms over you, but it might not result in actual death. Therefore, a situation of grave danger, such as a war zone, car crash, or industrial accident could all be considered as the shadow of death, even if you emerge unscathed.

Ultimately, whether you are in death's shadow due to imminent danger or terminal illness, this same Bible passage gives you hope. The author of the Psalms knew something that allowed him to "fear no evil." Like the psalmist, you too can fear no evil even in the fearful valley of the shadow of death. The truth about death will set your mind at ease and remove your fear.

Walking Through the Valley of the Shadow of Death

When you are in the shadow, look for the light.

The twenty-third Psalm is one of greatest pieces of literature ever penned. But more importantly, it is also God-inspired scripture that flowed from the heart of King David during a dark, painful time in his life. "Even though I walk through the valley of the shadow of death, I will fear no evil, for you are with me; your rod and your staff, they comfort me" (Ps. 23:4, ESV).

King David was experiencing a time of "doom and gloom"; he felt as though death was near. Dr Gordon Fair-Brain could relate to this Chapter of Psalms by King David very well because he too experienced hardship, peril, chaos, and deep suffering invading the whole of his life. In our fallen world, these things will invade our lives, too. Perhaps at some point, we will all make that long, slow, painful walk through the "valley of the shadow of death." In my life I have observed that most of the ungodly and diabolical individuals are incapable of empathising until it is their turn in the "valley of the shadow of death", and then they wish they had done things differently.

Here is a sobering thought if you may be walking in the valley right now—Yes, Dr Fair-Brain has been, the Council gave the doctor a damning and destructive report to please none other than their ego and their boss, the fallen Angel. This was based on something he could NOT control. <u>He was born black and could not change his colour but the 'white nurses' at the "Isle of White" felt he was the wrong colour to be working with them.</u> Apparently, they were too white and too superior to be working with him, an African born, black physician. If the GMC had been efficient and caring enough, they would have looked closely into the working relationship of the doctor and the White nurses to see if there was anything that deserved destroying the life of a caring. Compassionate and loving doctor.

Your valley could be something else. Maybe your spouse has left you? Or has your daughter decided to join ISIS? Has your child started using illicit drugs? Maybe your business has left you financially bankrupt? The enemy is always happy to hand you hurricanes or tornadoes.

No matter what the storm, it is so important that you and I remember a simple truth about the valley of the shadow of death. In order for there to be a shadow, there also must be a light.

And that light is Jesus, the great light of the world. Jesus walks in the valley with us. His light is also by our side. We are not alone. If you are not walking with Him, you are in darkness and capable of committing despicable atrocities.

Jesus is the light, but he is also the Great Shepherd, who walks with us and guides us. He will comfort us with his presence, even in the valley of the shadow of death.

"The Valley of the Shadow of Death"

I have been meditating on Psalm 23, particularly the verse that talks of walking through the Valley of the Shadow Death. In Israel there is a real Valley of the Shadow of Death. It is a steep, deep, and narrow canyon. The sun only hits the bottom of it when it is directly overhead at high noon. The rest of the time the bottom of the canyon is dark. David probably led his sheep through the valley of the shadow of death. As you look in the Bible, the term "valley" also refers several types of rough times in life.

- Joshua talks about the Valley of Calamity

- Job went through the Valley of Testing

- Moses talks about the Valley of Despair in the wilderness

- The Hebrew young men went through the Valley of Heat and hatred.

- Psalm 84 talks about the Valley of Weeping

- Hosea talks about the Valley of Trouble

- Jesus went through the Valley of Crucifixion and Death itself at the hands of the Religious Know-it-all's.

- The reference to a valley in Ps 23 in Hebrew means The Valley of Deep Darkness

Dr Fair-Brain, himself, in these narrative talks about <u>the Valley of Betrayal and Racial hatred.</u> What Valley are You going through today or have gone through?

This is what I find to be an immensely powerful thought. Up to this point in the Psalm, David has been speaking to the reader about God. David begins the Psalm, and says to the reader, hey let me tell you about the Lord. He is my Shepherd.

David then gets to the verse on the dark valleys of life, through which he has walked. He makes the statement, even though I walk through the valley of the Shadow of Death...and then he changes. He forgets the reader. He starts to speak to God. He says, "... for you are with me, your rod and staff they comfort me". The rest of the verse is talking to God.

It is as if David, as he was writing, started thinking about the tough times in his life; and while he was thinking he enters the presence of God. This experience is applicable to us as well. While we go through the deep valleys of life. The valleys of deep darkness cause us to enter the presence of God or to enter into deeper intimacy with God. In God's presence, His rod and staff will protect us from harm; and will guide us in the paths of righteousness.

Chapter #12

"HOPE FOR THE HOPELESS"

> Rejoice in the Lord always. I will say it again:
> Rejoice! Let your gentleness be evident to all.
> The Lord is near. Do not be anxious about any-
> thing, but in every situation, by prayer and peti-
> tion, with thanksgiving, present your requests to
> God. And the peace of God, which transcends all
> understanding, will guard your hearts and your
> minds in Christ Jesus. – Philippians 4:4-7 (NIV)

Everyone experiences periods of hopelessness in their lives. Whether it is the loss of a job, failing a class, a divorce or breakup, being kicked out of a home, the death of a loved one, whatever it may be – we have all been there. It is a part of being human. As a natural listener, I have heard many people unburden the weariness of their hearts to me, and I in turn have unburdened my troubles to others. Talking about the way we feel can sometimes be exceedingly difficult, but never have I known someone to feel worse after saying what they had been feeling inside. If anything, speaking about what our hearts are feeling helps us to heal, and sometimes, that is all we need.

However, expressing our thoughts and feelings to people alone will not bring about complete healing. This is not what brings us the peace and happiness we desire. We all long to have a purpose in life and a reason to hope. Without a purpose in life, and without a reason to hope, finding direction and motivation are difficult to find.

I (TG Fair-Brain) personally, have recently gone through a most trying time in my life where I felt completely hopeless, lost, and unmotivated. I did not care to live again. For the first two weeks after the most shocking verdict, I found myself unable to eat, unable to sleep, unable to concentrate on anything, or even speak about that shocking verdict. I started having difficulties resting and at times started having panic attacks. However, I was able to rediscover my sense of purpose when I gave my problems to God, my Father.

No reason to quit despite storms

I am a doctor who worked as Specialty Doctor in Medical Oncology; one who found himself in a very wrong working environment. After only two months at this one Hospital which I called the Isle of "White", I was reported to the Chief Medical Officer as being an incompetent doctor by **two White nurses**. I had worked in the United Kingdom for over fifteen years both in the Private and NHS TRUSTS but had never been labelled as incompetent. And this assessment was made in just two months of employment at this hospital by **two** "Caucasian" nurses – on this same **Isle of "White".** **But we know it was NOT incompetence but a skin-colour–Black.**

No friendly, comforting or encouraging word was ever spoken to me, and I never felt a sense of belonging from day one at this hospital. I felt unwanted, uncelebrated, and unimportant; and these people did nothing to show me that I was, in fact, wanted, important and a part of the team. I had hoped things would improve, but this was my fantasy dream. In fact, the reality of the situation became worse instead. It worsened until I was forced to resign. I left to maintain my sanity.

For two months I had placed my entire identity and happiness in other people. I trusted the nurses with whom I worked, and I initially felt that they were caring, loving and supportive people. I was in for a big surprise.

When your life is flanked by pain and suffering, it is normal to be filled with questions. Why is God allowing me to suffer like this? **Is He really in control of my life? Is He truly aware of what is going on in my life?** How can I possibly go on like this? "Does He really care"? But, in time, one will be reassured that God uses life's hurts to strengthen your faith for the future, and you will be comforted that all is never lost when your hope is in Christ.

When we place our self-worth in another human being, we are only setting ourselves up for a rude awakening. There is Only One who will never fail us, and that is our Father, God the Creator. We are always loved and cared for by Him. To Him, we are far more valuable than anything this universe has to offer us. I began to place all my burdens upon Him. I opened my heart back up to God. I really thought that my heart was open to Him, but I now know that it is impossible to place your self-worth in two places.

My identity had not been in God for a long time. After reopening my heart to God, I began to experience healing such as I had never experienced before. Light, hope, and peace began to flood into my heart. I still experience much pain, and often I feel sorrowful. Healing is possible, but it is by no means easy. At different times, I felt as if my heart were going to burst out of my chest. Because the emotional pain I felt would cause me great physical pain. I was often doubled over in great pain. I have shed buckets of tears late into the night. When I go to a GP, I still cry as I am explaining why I am not employed.

However, I continued to turn to God, and because of the hope I have in Him and His promises, it slowly but surely began to get easier and less painful. My sense of purpose and hope was renewed.

I praised God for His endless love and grace. I rejoiced in Him every day. When we look to God in times of trouble and continue to rejoice in Him during our troubles; instead of rejoicing in Him when everything in our lives is going well, we will find ourselves joyful and hopeful even in the most hopeless situations. Instead of feeling lost and without purpose, we find ourselves knowing exactly who we are, and where we are going. When we open our hearts to God and willingly go to Him in prayer, telling Him all of our troubles and problems, we will be granted a peace that transcends anything else we could ever experience. This is because we know that God, the creator of the universe, listens to us, cares for us, and always ready to be on our side as we go throughout life. We cannot fail with God at our side.

Over the last few weeks, I have found myself a much happier person than I ever have been in so many ways. There are so many things I can worry about: being a qualified medical doctor without a job, having a lot of monthly bills, not having money, having overseas missionary support suspended, and having my name now removed from the Medical Registry. God who allows difficulties for reasons we do not understand, but in His time we may understand. **God has been with Fair-Brain!**

God's goodness and love

There may appear to be so much uncertainty about the future, but I have discovered that worrying about things was not the solution. God's Word says, "Be anxious for nothing but in everything by prayer and supplication with thanksgiving let your requests be made known to God" (Phil 4:6). I am reminded that no matter what happens, I have a God who loves me and is always prepared to take care of me. Nothing has caught Him by surprise. God knew Satan would be allowed to torment me, but my Father has not forsaken or left me.

No matter what happens, I rejoice; because I have a glorious hope for my future that goes far beyond this world. The trials of this world are trivial in comparison to an eternity with the Father. This is the hope that I have, and God Himself is the source of the joy I experience daily. Often, I say these words with tears welling up in my eyes. I realize that there are many hurting people in the world, however it is my prayer that all people in the world will know the hope and joy God gives His people.

Finding Hope, Strength, and Comfort in Times of Trouble...

Each day has troubles. Sometimes the troubles are so great that we think they will break us. Unimaginable troubles...we never saw coming, hit us with such force, we are knocked down. Feeling weighed down, we look up, searching for help. God knows we will have troubled times such as these. He desires we place our hope in Him instead of our circumstances. In order to do that, we must have a healthy understanding of hope.

In Scripture, hope is a confident expectation for the future, describing both the act of hoping and the object hoped for. When grounded in God, hope provides the motivation to live the Christian life even in the face of trouble. With God there is hope, and where there is hope, there is confidence.

The Source of Hope

Despite all this, I will not utterly reject or despise them while they are in exile in the land of their enemies. I will not cancel my covenant with them by wiping them out. I the Lord, am their God. (Leviticus 26:44)

A Christian's hope is based on God's faithfulness. These verses show what God meant when he said he is slow to anger (Exodus 34:6). Even if the Israelites chose to disobey and were scattered among their enemies, God would still give them the opportunity to repent and return to him. His purpose was not to destroy them, but to help them grow.

Our day-to-day experiences and hardships are sometimes overwhelming; unless we can see that God's purpose is to bring about continual growth in us, we may despair. The hope we need is well expressed in Jeremiah 29:11-12: "For I know the plans I have for you,' says the Lord. 'They are plans for good and not for disaster, to give you a future and a hope. In those days when you pray, I will listen." Enduring hope as we suffer demonstrate that we understand God's mercy.

Where Do We Find Hope?

Jesus ignored their comments and said to Jairus, "Don't be afraid. Just trust me." (Mark 5:36)

Hope comes from trusting Christ. Jairus's crisis caused him to feel confusion, fear, and hopelessness. Jesus' words to Jairus during the crisis speak to us as well: "Don't be afraid. Just trust me." In Jesus' mind, there was both hope and promise. Each time you feel hopeless and afraid, look at your problem from Jesus' point of view. He is the source of all hope and promise.

We have been made right in God's sight by faith, we have peace with God because of what Jesus Christ our Lord has done for us, at the cross. God's faithfulness is the anchor of our faith.

Therefore, being justified by faith, we have peace with God through our Lord Jesus Christ: By whom also we have access by faith into this grace wherein we stand and rejoice in hope of the glory of God. (Romans 5:1-2)

Hope comes from remembering all that God has done for us. As Paul states clearly in 1 Cor. 13:13, faith, hope, and love are at the heart of the Christian life. Our relationship with God begins with faith. Hope grows as we learn all that God has in mind for us; it gives us the promise of the future. And God's love fills our life and gives us the ability to reach out to others.

Our Hope Grows During Difficult Times

Hope grows as we depend on God in the difficult times. For first-century Christians, suffering was the rule rather than the exception. Paul tells us that in the future we will become, but until then we must overcome. This means we will experience difficulties that help us grow. We rejoice in suffering not because we like pain or deny its tragedy, but because we know God is using life's difficulties and Satan's attacks to build our character. The problems that we run into will develop our perseverance—which in turn will strengthen our character, deepen our trust in God, and give us greater confidence about the future. You probably find your patience tested in some way every day. Thank God for those opportunities to grow, and deal with them in his strength (see also James 1:2-4; 1 Peter 1:6-7).

How do you remain hopeful during difficult times?

The Lord's Offer:

"Come unto Me, all you who labour and are heavy laden, and I will give you rest". "Take My yoke upon you and learn of Me... for I am meek and lowly in heart, and you shall find rest unto your souls". For My yoke is easy and My burden is light. (Matthew 11:28-30)

In Those difficult moments...

Remember, "Many are the afflictions of the righteous, but the Lord delivers him out of them all... " Psalm 34:19

We are told a true child of God will go through periods of trials, difficulties, pain, and suffering in this life. We may never know the "Why?" until we get to Heaven. Regardless of our age, intellect, responsibilities, or experience, in God's eyes we are still just little children. When we fall into various trials, God wants us to come to Him, to seek His Will and His direction, and to quit attempting to carry the burden ourselves. This requires faith. Jesus Christ stepped forth from eternity to become a man and to endure much pain, sorrow, rejection, grief, and excruciating physical trauma. Therefore, He knows what we are going through and how we feel. He loves and cares for each one of us and promises to help us through the difficult "storms" of life we are facing. Let's seek Jesus now and listen to His words of wisdom, instruction, and comfort...

"With A Little Faith…"

"Do not be afraid, nor be dismayed (distressed), for the Lord God is with you wherever you go." (Joshua 1:9)

"No matter how alone you might feel now… when you go through it all you will come through pure as gold", said Job.

"He (the Lord) will be with you; He will not leave you nor forsake you."(Deuteronomy 31:8)

"But without faith it is impossible to please Him, for he who comes to God must believe that He is, and that He is a rewarder of those who diligently seek Him."(Hebrews 11:6)

Pray honestly and sincerely seeking the Lord for direction…

"I, (the Lord) will instruct you and teach you in the way you should go" (Psalm 32:8).

"The righteous cry out, and the Lord hears and delivers them out of all of their troubles." (It sometimes takes a while though) (Psalm 34:17).

"We know that all things work together for good, to those who love God …" (Romans 8:28). Please note it says "…all things work together for good to those who love God …" even though we may never know the "How?" or "Why?" until we get to Heaven.)

It will not be easy, but no matter how bad things get or how long the storms last... we are instructed to TRUST in GOD!

"And those whose faith has made them good in God's sight must live by faith" (Hebrews 10:38)

Faith means trusting Him in EVERYTHING, every situation...We are commanded to trust Him in everything!

"Let your requests be made known to God, with thanksgiving, and the peace of God, which surpasses all understanding will guard your hearts and minds through Christ Jesus."(Philippians 4:6-7) Prayer point: Ask the Lord to have you feel as He would have you feel.

"If any of you lacks wisdom (concerning your situation), let him ask of God, who gives to all liberally and without reproach, and it will be given to him. But let him ask in faith, with NO doubting, for he who doubts is like a wave of the sea driven and tossed by the wind.

For let not that man (the man or woman who doubts God or God's Word) suppose that he will receive anything from the Lord"(James 1:5-7)

We need to let go of the past (including yesterday). "Forgetting (completely and absolutely) that which lies behind and reaching forward to what lies ahead." (Philippians 3:13). I have highlighted this because I just want to say, Paul wrote those words to remind us that when we allow our past to bleed into our present this will pollute our future.

Prayer point: Ask the Lord for help forgetting the pains, the failures, and the fears from the past. I have heard it said that an axe soon forgets the chopping it did to a tree, but the tree never forgets the pain and hurt it felt while being chopped. In this author's life, the axe is The Diabolical Medical Association (DMA) may have long forgotten the actions which altered the author's life, but the tree (which is the author himself) has not. Ask in your prayer for God's help for Forgetting the past hurts, glories, and achievements. Move on day by day, in faith, towards God.

When your heart and mind are troubled...

"Fix your thoughts on Him whatever things are true, whatever things are noble, whatever things are just, whatever things are pure, whatever things are lovely, whatever things are of good report, if there is any virtue and if there is anything praise-worthy -meditate on these things." (Philippians 4:8)

Note: Do not focus your thoughts on the problem or hurt! Dwelling on the problem will only make things worse. Somebody has put it this way that focussing on your burden will make you miss your blessing. With a thankful heart dwell on all those things God has blessed you with ... and focus on the hope and the promises found in Jesus Christ (**Yeshua Ha'Mashiach in Hebrew**) to help you through these painful periods (step-by-step ... and day-by-day).

I like what Joel Osteen said, "God allows the burden on us because He trusts that we can endure it before the blessing. It is Not usually the reverse". The problem is when we have a burden, we focus on it so much that we miss the Blessing in it. The Bigger the Burden, the more Highly you have been favoured. Anybody can do easy things. Mary, the Mother of Jesus, was highly favoured and other young women were envious of her, but they forgot that she had a very Big Burden to carry. She was about to get married to Joseph but suddenly she is pregnant; how would she explain the pregnancy without a man? How would Joseph feel? What would the people think?"

Many times, we want roses without thorns, gain without pain, power without the Cross and Pay without Work.

"Trust in the LORD with all your heart, and lean not on your own understanding"(Proverbs 3:5)

Remember, He warned us there will be great difficulties in this life ... but He promises great Rewards for all who will place their trust in Him and faithfully endure the painful trials and afflictions which will come upon us during this short life.

God answers all prayers from those who diligently seek Him (many times the Answer may be "Yes". At other times He may say "Not yet". There will be times that the answer is "No". Please remember it's His Will we seek, not our will, His time, not our time, and His Way, not our way. Only God knows the end from the beginning. Do not be discouraged when prayers are not answered exactly the way we want or when we want. He genuinely cares and knows what is best. I heard one wise man say, "Not every open door is yours…"

Remember, the Lord Jesus Christ is the good Shepherd, for "The good shepherd gives his life for the sheep ...". He has prepared a narrow path of safety for each of us through this life. Although His path might appear the most difficult, it is the only one which will lead us safely home into His Kingdom of Heaven. It will seem overwhelming at times, but we must trust in Him. Without Him we are lost. Seek His direction, then walk in faith.

"So, take a new grip with your tired hands, stand firm on your shaky legs, and mark out a straight, smooth path for your feet so that those who follow you, though weak and lame, will not fall and hurt themselves, but become strong..."(Hebrews 12:12)

"With A Little Hope..."

"The Angel of the Lord camps around (guards and protects) those who fear Him. Blessed is the man or woman who trusts in Him." (Psalm 34:7,8)

"The Lord is near to those who have a broken heart and saves those who have a humbled (contrite) spirit. "Many are the afflictions of the righteous, but the Lord delivers him out

of them all." (We are made righteous when we ask Jesus into our lives...). (Psalm 34:19)

Even the sincerest Christian will not escape the pain, heartbreak, sorrow, and distress found in this life, but the Lord promises to help us, to strengthen us, and to see us through it all. His promise is not to take us out of the bitter storms of life, but to safely lead us through the storms. Therefore, no matter how bad the situation might seem now, it will one day be over and behind you. Trust in Him.

"The eye of the Lord is on those who fear Him, on those who hope in His mercy... our soul waits for the Lord." Like me, some of you feel God has the habit of turning His back on those He loves. We question His love, because He claims He loves us, but we do not understand why there are so many tornadoes, hurricanes, and turbulent storms. **It appears to us that those who curse and mock Him, seem to be blessed. A young man kicking around a ball filled with hot air is paid <£200 million while a doctor's current balance in his bank is about £10.** Yes. I am a doctor that has blessed God's people for over fifteen years here in the United Kingdom, but this has been my bank account balance has been quite low for a long time.

Waiting is hard, especially when we feel the battle between our faith and our fears, anger, anxieties, or pain is raging inside of us.

"Job is an example of a man who continued to trust the Lord in sorrow and suffering. Even through his suffering and affliction we can see how the Lord's plan finally ended in good... for the Lord is full of tenderness and mercy."

Even the book of Job shows God sovereignty over all things, including the terrible things which happened to Job, by Satan. It was Satan's desire that Job would listen to his wife, and "to curse God and die." In each trial we go through we have the choice of drawing closer to the Lord in faith, or bitterly turning away to "curse God and die." This is the test.

The road to Heaven is not an easy one as God tests our faith along the way... "Because narrow is the gate and Difficult is the way which leads to life (in Heaven), and there are few who find it." (Ask

Jesus into your heart and you will find it). (Matthew 7:14) "Count it all joy when you fall into various trials (difficulties), knowing that the testing of your faith develops patience.

But let patience have its perfect work, that you might be perfect and complete, lacking nothing." (James 1:2-4)

The "trials" and "tests" in life are not joyful, but when they are over, we find joy in knowing the Lord absolutely loves us and as a loving Father helps us develop the patience, obedience, and humility we need to grow and walk-in faith...

"And have you forgotten the exhortation (the encouraging words) which God speaks to you as sons (and daughters)? He said... 'My son do not despise the chastening of the Lord, nor be discouraged when you are rebuked by Him.

For whom the Lord loves He chastens and scourges every son whom He receives.'

For if you endure chastening, God deals with you as sons (and daughters) for what son is there whom a father does not chasten?" (Hebrews 12:5-7)

"Now, no chastening seems to be joyful for the present, but painful, nevertheless, afterward it yields the peaceable

fruit of righteousness to those who have been trained by it."
(Hebrews 12:11)

Not all trials are from chastening. We may never know the
reason until we get to Heaven. But sufferings in the life of
the believer helps God conform us into His image; and helps
us to become more like Him in patience, gentleness, kind-
ness, humility, compassion, forgiveness, and obedience. Faith
increases strength and power.

Cling to God's promises during the storms ...

"Do NOT worry (or be anxious) about anything, but pray
about everything... with thanksgiving"(Philippians 4:6) (Did
you know this is a commandment?) "Do NOT be anxious for
tomorrow, for tomorrow will care for itself." (Matthew 6:34)

"Therefore, whoever hears these sayings of mine, and does
them, I will liken him to a wise man who built his house on the
rock: and the rain descended, the floods came, and the winds
blew and beat

on that house, and it did not fall, for it was founded on the
Rock." (Jesus is the Rock who will help and strengthen us.)
(Matthew 7:24-25)

Fear No One or Nothing but God...

"For God has NOT given us a spirit of FEAR"(2 Timothy 1:7)

... for fear is not of the Spirit of the Lord. The root of fear eats away like a worm and produces pain, anger, jealousy, depression, neurosis, bitterness, and guilt. Do not fear! But by the same token, it is prudent to retain a little bit of fear that will make you cautious and not get careless.

Please remember...

God loves you more than words can say. He knows the pain and heartbreak we feel ... for He has felt it, too. The Bible says our spirit will someday groan to leave this earthly body. Our real life, in His Kingdom of Heaven, is yet future... "The Spirit Himself bears witness with our spirit

that we are children of God, and if children, then heirs — heirs of God and joint heirs with the Messiah (Christ), If indeed we suffer with Him" (Romans 8:16)

Jesus (Yeshua) is our Hope...

Although there are times we may feel alone and abandoned, He will never forsake you or leave you. The Bible says the true child of God will find suffering in this life. Each of us will have our faith tested. Jesus waits for us to ask Him into our lives to help, to strengthen, to comfort, and to heal. He lovingly wraps His arms around the lonely and the broken-hearted.

Jesus will never cast away or turn away any man or woman that willingly comes to Him, regardless of how young or how old, or how good or how bad. All who come to Him with a sincere and humbled heart are welcomed with open arms. "If God is for us, who can be against us?" (Romans 8:31). Jesus is God.

He now prepares our place in Heaven where there will be no fear, no worries, no pain, no heartbreak, and no tears. He will see you through these difficult times... Trust in Him!

Your Hope in Times of Suffering

However difficult your situation may be – however much 'trouble' you are facing in your life, you can have hope. Hope is the confident expectation of God's ultimate blessing in this life and the life to come, based upon the goodness and promises of God. With Jesus, there is always hope (Job).

Hope is the ultimate triumph of good over evil (Psalm 64:1-10).

Do you ever feel terrified by something you are facing in your life? (Yes! The evil, hateful and manipulative GMC, and its intimidations of young doctors.) David faced 'the terror of the enemy'

He (Fair-Brain) went through times of real terror, 'the conspirators set out to get him' (v.2, MSG), 'evil plans', conniving, (v.5a) and 'traps' (v.5b, MSG). Yet, he was confident that God would triumph over evil. What should we do when we face similar troubles? The psalm today gives us some clues:

• Cry out to God

David prays, 'Listen and help, O God' (v.1a, MSG). David asks God: 'protect my life from the threat of the enemy. (v.1b).

• 'Rejoice in the Lord'

'Rejoice in the Lord' (v.10a). As the apostle Paul puts it, 'Rejoice in the Lord always. I will say it again: Rejoice!' (Philippians 4:4).

• Stay close to the Lord

'Take refuge in him' (Psalm 64:10b). 'Fly to God' (v.10b, MSG).

• Keep praising God

'Let all the upright in heart praise him!' (v.10c). 'Make praise your habit' (v.10c, MSG).

Prayer point: Lord, thank you that I can be confident of the ultimate triumph of good over evil. Thank you that you go with me into the battles. Thank you that I am never alone. Lord, I praise you.

Hope in the resurrection of Jesus

Do you fear death? Many people are afraid of death. But if you put your faith in Jesus, you do not need to fear death. Jesus has defeated the power of death. Russell Brand (the English comedian, actor, columnist, singer, author and presenter) said, **'Laughter is addictive because of the inevitability of death. It**

<u>gives us a temporary escape – for the moment it stops the fear of the inevitability of death.</u> 'Every human being will face the 'trouble' of death. Where does your hope lie?

In this book, we see the full humanity of Jesus in the face of death. Lazarus was his friend. Jesus loved him (v.3). He was 'deeply moved' and 'troubled' by his death (v.33). In the shortest verse in the Bible we read, 'Jesus wept' (v.35).

Yet Jesus is also, uniquely, the answer to death. Jesus said to Martha, "Your brother will be raised up." Martha replied, "I know that he will be raised up in the resurrection at the end of time." "You don't have to wait for the End. I am, right now, Resurrection and Life. The one who believes in me, even though he or she dies, will live. And everyone who lives believing in me does not ultimately die at all'" (vv.24–26, MSG).

There is life beyond the grave. Jesus died and rose again. Everyone who believes in Jesus will rise again from the dead. As a foretaste of the future, Jesus raises Lazarus from the dead. Bishop Leslie Newbiggin was once asked, 'Are you an optimist or a pessimist?' He said, 'I'm neither – Jesus Christ is risen from the dead.' Jesus healed many of His people and He died for them, then in three days he rose from the dead; this left us resurrection power.

We are neither optimists nor pessimists – rather, we are hopeful. We have a completely certain hope. The resurrection of Jesus Christ is the basis of our future hope.

This resurrection power also belongs to the church. Paul writes to the church of Rome, 'If the Spirit of him who raised Jesus from the dead is living in you, he who raised Christ from the dead will also give life to your mortal bodies because of his Spirit who lives in you' (Romans 8:11).

Christianity is the largest movement of all time. It is the only one that never loses a member through death. I remember one of my sons, when he was a little boy, saying, 'When you die, I'll be sad. Then I'll see you in heaven and I won't be sad anymore!' He didn't know what he was saying but that was the truth.

Mother Teresa was asked shortly before her death, 'Are you afraid of dying?' She said, 'How can I be? Dying is going home to God. I have never been afraid. No, on the contrary,' she said, 'I am really looking forward to it!'

This also indirectly provides a picture of hope for the church. There is a sickness in parts of the church. Some parts of the church seem to have 'fallen asleep' (John 11:11). And in some cases, there seems to be a 'bad odour' (v.39).

This also reminds us of Jesus' power to bring even the dead to life. This resurrection power is still at work in the true church of Christ today. The same Jesus who said over Lazarus 'this sickness will not end in death' (v.4), also promised that he would 'build [His] Church, and the gates of Hell shall not prevail against it' (Matthew 16:18, KJV).

Some parts of the church seem to have been prematurely buried. Jesus said about Lazarus, 'Take off the grave clothes and let him go' (John 11:44c). Maybe Jesus would say something similar to some of the churches today.

Prayer point: Lord, I pray for the church. Forgive us where we have fallen asleep and are giving off a bad odour. Thank you that we know you are deeply moved by the situation, that you weep over the church, and that you will act out of love. May the sickness of the church not end in death.

Lord, would you bring new life. I pray for an end to church closures and decline. May we see the church come alive all over the world.

Hope in the word of GOD!

Do you realise that God wants to speak to you? You can say, like the Old Testament prophet Samuel, "Speak Lord, for your servant is listening". First Samuel 3:10

These were times of trouble for the people of God. They cried out, 'We're in trouble!' (4:3). It was a time when it seemed that God was almost silent. 'In those days, the word of the Lord was rare; there were not many visions. It must have been heart breaking for Eli to see his own sons dishonouring the Lord. They slept with the women who served at the entrance to the Tent of Meeting. They dishonoured God who has said, 'Those who honour me I will honour, but those who despise me will be disdained'. As a result of the dishonouring of God, the people of God are defeated (4:1b–11). Eli dies heartbroken (vv.12–18). His daughter-in-law gave birth to a son, whom she named Ichabod; which means "The glory has departed".

Yet, in the midst of these terrible times of trouble for the people of God there is hope. The Lord called Samuel. God revealed himself to Samuel, and he listened to the Lord. He said, "Speak, God. I'm your servant, ready to listen". The Lord replied, "See, I am about to do something in Israel that will make the ears of everyone who hears of it tingle".

Samuel was prepared to pass on the message in its entirety, however unpopular, embarrassing, and difficult it was. He did not hide anything. As a result, God was able to use him greatly: "The Lord was with Samuel as he grew up, and he let none of his words fall to the ground".

Prayer point: Lord, help me to follow the example of Samuel and pray daily in my heart, 'Speak, Lord, for your servant is listening'. Help me to listen carefully to the word of God and then pass it on without altering it to please my audience.

I am now destined for the Grape land -the PROMISE LAND, Praise my Lord Jesus Christ! Amen!

Chapter #13

"I CAN DO ALL THINGS THROUGH CHRIST ..." Philippians 4:13 NKJV

A t the writing of this book (more thirty-six months after the Verdict from the GMC) I have been floundering in the wilderness and in the valleys of the shadow of death. All who have ever been there, know the terrain; the wilderness is an inhospitable, an uncomfortable, and an unpleasant environment.

Sometimes you become so accustomed to dark places that light becomes foreign to you. You get so used to dark valleys that mountain-top experience is foreign. In my opinion, translational thinking will undo the familiarity with darkness of the valley and will make the mountain-top experience less foreign. Translational thinking will mean nothing if there is no of action. Translational thinking leads to translational action.

When I came up against the General Medical Council for the fabricated allegations from the Isle of "White & Hurt", **Honesty and Truth were my only offensive and defensive weapons, because that was all I knew.** The GMC focussed on the spurious accusations and pointed their racial fingers at me, as if I was the dishonest one. I was the one failed by the wicked system. When I said the Truth, they tried to force me into saying the opposite (Untruth) for which they labelled me as "lacking insight". They wanted to conclude I was psychotic, which of course, I would not admit because I was not. I am not. The two psychiatrists confirmed I was not psychotic.

At the moment, my financial status is still in ruins. It is so bad, that I have been forced to have one meal a day; because that is all I could afford. I started frequenting the Lidl grocery shops (food is cheapest here). Our lives have been changed for ever by the GMC/MPTS who are supposed to be helping and supporting doctors of this country. **The GMC is destroying doctors with no remorse. In fact, it seems that they are more pleased if it's another black doctor who has taken his life, because of the evil treatment of the hateful, racial, and manipulative Council.** I had been labelled by the GMC "a risk to the public and patients," Frankly, I still do not know whom I was a risk. **My simple prayer to God is that "One of these days, their eyes will be opened to see the Truth."**

I honestly feel they tried to kill me with anxiety, stress, feelings of failure and guilt. However, my resilience was strong against the evil treatment I received. The unfair erasure of my medical license would not be the cause of my death, had been my resolve. I had no income; therefore, I could not provide for my immediate family; I could not help my extended family members. I could not continue support of a missionary project. Before the unfair erasure of my license, I was able to support, destitute African families left destitute by HIV and other tropical illnesses.

The truth is that the Council needs to be investigated; something is wrong with an organisation which cannot tell the difference between <u>"RIGHT</u> and <u>WRONG"</u>. Our government is allowing a wicked organisation to be in charge of doctors, yet the doctors are randomly censured, in my opinion. Prayerfully there will be someone who cares enough, someone with the power to investigate the council. Then through discovery those who are wicked and dangerous, will be exposed. The British need and deserve the best medical treatment from their government. The current pandemic and its demands on the doctors and nurses, should have proven to those in the council the importance of supporting and encouraging doctors like Dr Fair-Brain, who just needed caution and encouragement. COVID-19 did not discriminate and did not target any people group. The council responsible for the ending of Dr Fair-Brain's employment should be under review, especially at this time when all the doctors we have are needed. COVID-19, for British medicine is a fortunate stroke of serendipity. COVID-19 has distanced and terminated and overworked many doctors and nurses. Again, prayerfully the council will relent its spurious attacks in the aftermath of the worldwide pandemic. In fact, when Brexit is fully implemented, it will take longer to get the medical staff needed to maintain health in the United Kingdom.

Nonetheless, the Council intimidates the accused and their so called 'witnesses' are given false information during what they call the "investigation". Their solicited witnesses are skilled in lying, perversion of justice and are expert manipulators supporting the Council in its destruction of caring, loving, and competent doctors especially if they are Black. My heart screams in me, "Please. Somebody wake up and smell the coffee, this GMC is a destructive machinery."

The GMC will either ignore or conduct a cursory investigation on the behaviour of local Caucasian professionals who do as they please in hospitals such as 'carving their signatures of patients' organs. These doctors escape with some light warning. God help us!

I went to medical school for about nine years, to become a professional who would pursue a career I love. Instead, I have been granted a Verdict of termination of my career by an organisation that masquerades as a protector of the public and patients. When in fact, the council are the ones causing harm to the public. The council should encourage and protect their doctors as much as possible. **"GMC working with doctors for the patients"** is their motto as seen on their stationery, **but this is not TRUE. I would agree if they said, "GMC working with local <u>'White' doctors for patients".**</u>

The GMC believes they are closing wounds of colour discrimination and prejudice when they are actually opening wider the wounds of this Pandemic Racism. The GMC do not respect <u>Honesty or Truth</u>. They honour their own twisted honesty and their definition of truth. Sane individuals living

in this century who genuinely care about humanity should do everything possible to **Destroy the Pandemic Racism, Discrimination, and Hatred.** Supporting the latter is of Satan; it is Not Godly.

We serve a Mighty and Extraordinary God. He has an extraordinary Calling on some of His children, **in earlier chapters we learnt that their Opposition may appear extraordinarily insurmountable. Remember! NO human being can STOP the plans of Almighty GOD; and by trying to do so, one will find oneself in direct opposition with Him and one surely will NOT win.** I can guarantee you that. If you please God, He will take care of your enemies, haters, and all those not excited with seeing you fulfil your Calling from Him. **Like me you might have been setback for a Great comeback.**

Paul writes, **"I can do all things through Christ who strengthens me."** That means I can change, and I can be different. I can still fulfil my Calling. I long stopped setting myself up for failure by constantly criticising myself: 'I'm no good. I am a loser; the Wicked GMC is right, or I simply can never be a good doctor, and have no control over my life.' Instead, I say, **'Everything is possible for him who believes'** (Mark 9:23). 'And I believe I am an Overcomer; I am Empowered; I am Anointed; I am Intelligent; I am Victorious. I believe No Weapon formed against me by the enemy shall prosper; and I believe that Every Tongue that shall rise (or has risen up) in Judgement against me shall be condemned..." Before this Word, He said He is the same one who created the same individual carrying the weapon to attack me. **My GOD is a Very BIG GOD; He is Sovereign. He oversees you and me.** We both cannot win opposing each other. **Darkness and Light cannot live in the same house; one must give in.** I am in the light; I will leave it to you the reader to figure out where GMC is. Do not worry a crowd can be very wrong.

Chapter #14

GOD'S ABSOLUTE SOVEREIGNTY

Psalm 115:3; Isaiah 46:10; Jonah 2:9; John 6:65;
Romans 8:28–30; Romans 9:15–21; Romans
11:36; Ephesians 1:14-11; Titus 1:1; 1 Peter 1:1-2

N o doctrine is more despised by the natural
mind than the Absolutely sovereignty of God.
Human pride loathes the suggestion that God orders
everything, controls everything, rules over everything.
The carnal mind, burning with enmity against God,
abhors the Biblical teaching that nothing comes to
pass except according to His eternal decrees. Most of
all, the flesh hates the notion that salvation is entirely
God's work. If God chose who would be saved, and
if His choice was settled before the foundation of the
world, then believers deserve no credit for their salvation. **Haters of humanity have their destiny decided
already just like all workers of iniquity who decided**

the doctor was not fit to practice medicine because he was <u>Black</u>.

God declares "the end from the beginning...saying, 'My purpose will be established, and I will accomplish all My good pleasure'" (Isaiah 46:10). He is not subject to others' decisions. His purposes for choosing some and rejecting others are hidden in the secret counsels of His own will.

Moreover, everything that exists in the universe exists, because God allowed it, decreed it, and called it into existence. **"Our God is in the heavens; He does whatever He pleases"**. "Whatever the Lord pleases, He does, in heaven and in earth, in the seas and in all deeps". He **"works all things after the counsel of His will"**. "From Him and through Him and to Him are all things". "For us there is but one God, the Father, from whom are all things, and we exist for Him; and one Lord, Jesus Christ, by whom are all things, and we exist through Him". In accordance with His sovereignty, **He has a special place reserved for haters of humanity called eternity in the Lake of fire.**

What about sin? God is not the author of sin, but He certainly has allowed it. Sin is integral to His eternal decree. God has a purpose for allowing it. He cannot be blamed for evil or tainted by its existence; "There is no one holy like the Lord". But He certainly was not caught off-guard or standing helpless to stop it when sin entered the universe. We do not know His purposes for allowing sin. If nothing else, He permitted it to destroy evil forever. And God sometimes uses evil to accomplish good (Genesis 45:7, 50:20; Romans 8:28). How can these things be?

Scripture does not answer all the questions for us. But we know from His Word that God is utterly sovereign, He is perfectly holy, and He is just. GMC, UK is not.

Admittedly, those truths are hard for the human mind to embrace, but Scripture is unequivocal. God controls all things, right down to choosing who will be saved. Paul states the doctrine in inescapable terms in the ninth chapter of Romans, by showing that God chose Jacob and rejected his twin brother Esau "though the twins were not yet born, and had not done anything good or bad, in order that God's purpose according to His choice might stand, not because of works, but because of Him who calls". A few verses later, Paul adds this: "He says to Moses, 'I will have mercy on whom I have mercy, and I will have compassion on whom I have compassion.' So, then it does not depend on the man who wills or the man who runs, but on God who has mercy".

Paul anticipated the argument against divine sovereignty: "You will say to me then, 'Why does He still find fault? For who resists His will?'". In other words, doesn't God's sovereignty cancel out human responsibility? But rather than offering a philosophical answer or a deep metaphysical argument, Paul simply reprimanded the sceptic: "On the contrary, who are you, O man, who answers back to God? The thing moulded will not say to the moulder, 'Why did you make me like this,' will it? Or does not the potter have a right over the clay, to make from the same lump one vessel for honourable use, and another for common use?"

Scripture affirms both divine sovereignty and human responsibility. We must accept both sides of the truth, though we may not understand how they correspond to one another. People are responsible for what they do with the gospel—or with whatever light they have, so that punishment is just if they reject the light. And those who reject do so voluntarily. Some people actually choose to be wrong consciously. Jesus lamented, "You are unwilling to come to Me, that you may have life". He told unbelievers, "Unless you believe that I am [God], you shall die in your sins" (John 8:24).

Above all, we must not conclude that God is unjust because He chooses to bestow grace on some, but not to everyone. God is never to be measured by what seems fair to human judgment. Are we so foolish as to assume that we who are fallen, sinful creatures have a higher standard of what is right than an unfallen and infinitely, eternally holy God? What kind of pride is that? In Psalm 50:21 God says, "You thought that I was just like you." But God is not like us, nor can He be held to human standards. "My thoughts are not your thoughts, neither are your ways My ways,' declares the Lord. 'For as the heavens are higher than the earth, so are My ways higher than your ways, and My thoughts than your thoughts" (Isaiah 55:8-9).

We step out of bounds when we conclude that anything God does is not fair. In Romans 11:33 the apostle writes, "Oh, the depth of the riches both of the wisdom and knowledge of God! How unsearchable are His judgments and unfathomable His ways! For who has known the mind of the Lord, or who became His counsellor?" (Romans 11:33–34).

What does it mean, God is sovereign?

Answer: God's sovereignty is one of the most important principles in Christian theology, as well as one of its most hotly debated. Whether or not God is sovereign is usually not a topic of debate; all mainstream Christian sects agree that God is preeminent in power and authority. **God's sovereignty is a natural consequence of His omniscience, omnipotence, and omnipresence.**

God is described in the Bible as all-powerful and all-knowing, outside of time, and responsible for the creation of everything. These divine traits set the minimum boundary for God's sovereign control in the universe, which is to say that nothing in the universe occurs without God's permission. God has the power and knowledge to prevent anything He chooses to prevent, so (Please Note) anything that does happen must, at the very least, be "allowed" by God. **What GMC did or is doing to innocent doctors of colour does not go unnoticed by Almighty God, and He may allow it for reasons that will backfire.**

At the same time, the Bible describes God as offering humanity choices, holding them personally responsible for their sins, and being unhappy with some of their actions. The fact that sin exists at all proves that not all things that occur are the direct actions of God, who is holy. The reality of human volition (and human accountability) sets the maximum boundary for God's sovereign control over the universe, which is to say there is a point at which God chooses to allow things that He does not directly cause. When God allows a group of men and women to judge unfairly over His chosen people, He will come back with vengeance. He said, 'vengeance is mine; I shall repay…' In other words, He retaliates on our behalf.

The fact that God is sovereign essentially means that He has the power, wisdom, and authority to do anything He chooses within His creation. Whether or not He actually exerts that level of control in any given circumstance is actually a completely different question. Often, the concept of divine sovereignty is oversimplified. We tend to assume that, if God is not directly, overtly, purposefully driving some event, then He is somehow not sovereign. The cartoon version of sovereignty depicts a God who must do anything that He can do, or else He is not truly sovereign.

If a man were to put an ant in a bowl, the "sovereignty" of the man over the ant is not in doubt. The ant may try to crawl out, and the man may not want this to happen. But the man is not forced to crush the ant, drown it, or pick it up. The man, for reasons of his own, may choose to let the ant crawl away, but the man is still in control. There is a difference between allowing the ant to leave the bowl and helplessly watching as it escapes.

The cartoon version of God's sovereignty implies that, if the man is not actively holding the ant inside the bowl, then he must be unable to keep it in there at all. We are all like ants in His sight, so for a moment imagine all He can do with us. As He pleases...as he chooses. That is the sovereign will of God.

This illustration of the man and the ant is a miniscule parallel of God's sovereignty over mankind. God can do anything, to act and intervene in any situation, but He often chooses to act indirectly or to allow certain things for reasons of His own. When Dr Fair-Brain was treated unfairly by the Isle of "White" Hospital and the General Medical Council, God could have intervened and stop the cruelty and harshness of the investigation. His will is unimpeded, in any case. God's "sovereignty" means that He is absolute in authority and unrestricted in His supremacy. Everything that happens is, at the very least, the result of God's permissive will. This holds true even if certain specific things are not what He would prefer. The right of God to allow mankind's free choices is just as necessary for true sovereignty as His ability to enact His will, wherever and however He chooses.

Chapter #15

THE SPIRITUAL TRANQUILIZER IN TURBULENT TIMES.

H ave you experienced troubled times? Have you ever been at the place of "NO HOPE"? No one will ever know the Love, the care and compassion of Almighty God until they have stood at this place of NO HOPE or this lonely place where 'You Stand Alone'.

My home environment is not the best; my focus is temporarily distorted. We are going from day to day wondering what the next day will bring. I have been living on one meal a day. I have asked God to confirm I was still on the right road. The enemy has thrown a curve ball on me lately hence the confusion and request for my whereabouts.

I go to sleep, and middle of the night I wake up to voices streaming through my mind, "He is not responding to your prayers; He has forgotten about you, and you will not make it…" Of course, I block them and tell the evil one where to go and how to get there. Does he listen though? Surely, he does not, because a few minutes later another voice comes knocking at the portal of entry of my mind again with another negative word.

My work situation has been derailed by the emissaries of the Chief of Darkness despite all that I did for His children. I decided to handle the situation by just sitting down, in the corner somewhere, and waiting on Him. I reminded Him, of His Word, He said He would never leave me nor forsake me, and what He started He said He would complete. GOD can do exceedingly abundantly above and beyond what you and I can ever imagine or even think.

In troubled times I discovered that it is NOT time to keep looking at the Mountain because it will not move. I look at GOD to move the mountain. I do not blame anybody for my giants or mountains; I simply chose to trust and believe in GOD. He is bigger than the mountain. Staring at it will not make it move or change location and size.

It is said, "Satan has many tools, but deception is the handle that fits them all". One of these lies is when people believe they are in Total Control, and they really are not. GMC is not in complete control of my destiny ~ God is.

My Spiritual Legal Adviser finally gave me the advice that I needed, and that has given me Peace that Passes ALL Understanding, or you could say I received "The tranquilizer for my troubled times". He said, "The things that were meant for evil, the Lord turned them into good..." (Genesis 50:20). What was meant for a disappointment for Dr Fair-Brain will turn out to be an appointment.

Things happen sometimes that we cannot explain. It is during those times, I discovered that I needed to believe and trust my GOD. I heard one lady say we should Not Only Trust but Obey as well. God's delays are Not denials.

It was very hurtful and disappointing for me with dark clouds crossing my horizon, feelings of hatred for my situation welling up in my spirit, and questions bombarding my mind that I could not answer, and everything seemed to spell "NO HOPE". But I had to dig deep and believe GOD, because He said, "When you (Dr Fair-Brain) pass through the waters I will be with you... they shall not overflow you. When you walk through the fire... it shall not consume you". GOD has a promise for every trial, test, need, storm, or circumstance in life. I have FAITH in GOD because He is BIGGER than my circumstances. His decisions are better than those made by human judicial courts. GOD appoints, and Satan disappoints. When you or I hurt others, especially GOD's own, we can count on God's vengeance against us.

I am proud to be a believer in Almighty GOD, and I do not apologise for praying with or for my patients. I am a Servant of GOD masquerading as a physician. The more we understand and love the Lord the less we will focus on self.

I do not have to worry about trying to explain my circumstances and to understand why. You may ask, "Is it because I have such great faith?" No, I have little faith in a BIG GOD, despite moments of quietness towards me. It is not so much the amount of FAITH as the object of my faith that counts. It is not what I believe, but WHO I believe in. All that I am and all that I do is because of the sovereignty of God. There is NO ONE is above reproach including you reader. Our titles and position in this world are ordained by God alone. It is our responsibility to remember God's sovereignty in the whole of our lives. I hope you have heard it said, **"There is no failure more dangerous than success that leaves GOD out".**

I trust GOD because He never fails me. He said, "Put No Trust in man because man will fail you…" Not surprisingly, I have been failed by many people whom I trusted very much.

You and I are GOD's children, but we differ in who or what we put our faith in. If I put faith in my job, qualifications or what I believe I have accomplished, all this will fail me. So, I choose to put FAITH in GOD who never fails and will never LIE to ME. GOD is the giver of opportunities that we all have whether as employer or employee. He can also take away from us, at any moment, anything we think we own. His Word says, 'It is He who gives power to get wealth…' **Our beliefs must align with His Word because Truth is indisputable.** Many non-believers started trusting in God when we had the recent COVD-19 pandemic because they did not know to whom to turn. I choose to trust GOD; He has given all of us freedom of choice.

The worst thing, in life, is not poverty of material things but poverty of spiritual things. Spiritual poverty, simply put,

is life without God's love, without God's redemption, and without God's salvation. With our free will, we may choose to be spiritually impoverished. Spiritual poverty affects us all, and not knowing one's destiny and destination is merely the symptom. Any individual is deprived of understanding and blessings of life, because of spiritual poverty. Those who are on a journey without knowledge of where they are headed will not know when they have arrived, at their destination. In fact, they may not know what their destiny is nor who is in controls.

"No human" controls my destiny; GOD and I control my destiny. God controls my destiny by His sovereignty, but I control my destiny by trusting and obeying God. If my GOD destined for me to succeed, no one else will change that. I believe it is narrow-minded of anybody claiming to be 'Chief-of-whatever' to believe they can decide whether I fail or succeed. That is delusional. Only God has the authority to distribute talents and gifts to His creation.

Losing a job because somebody did not like me or maybe because of my (Black) colour, ethnic background; or because I pray for or with my patients is allowed in God's sovereign plan for me, as a child of God and is a very minor issue for me. If it were because I had been impolite or uncompassionate to my patients; that would have certainly disturbed me. **Patients are more than just objects of our own exploitation; they are Tripartite Beings with the Soul, Spirit and Physical and in treating them for their diseases we must remember that they were created in God's own image.** Therefore, we are to treat them as we, ourselves, would like to be treated, since this is the command of God's word. Of course, Only ignorance tells you that a diseased body is only managed by physical modalities.

Who controls your destiny? Do you understand my question? Prayerfully, you do know the answer to my question, It matters that you know your destiny, your destination, and that God is in control of all. In that case, all you need to do is trust and obey, God Himself. In either case, the final destination can be pleasant or unpleasant; it will be pleasant if you trust and obey, but it will be unpleasant is you mistrust and disobey. Understand that you have a destination towards which you are fast approaching where you will be answerable for ALL that you have done in destroying or building His people. Destinations can be pleasant depending on where you end up. There is an end destination for all, whether you have chosen to be a believer or a non-believer.

We now go from spiritual poverty to spiritual blindness. Physical blindness, again, is not the worst disadvantage but spiritual blindness is. Physical blindness causes one to miss the sunlight, the rainbows the smile and even the frowns around oneself. On the other hand, spiritual blindness causes one neither can see nor understand the world around them, the world seen and unseen. Simply, the unseen world is the spiritual world. The seen world includes the sunrises, sunsets and rainbows in the clouds. The spiritually blind a very handicapped, for they cannot see beyond their noses; all they see is I, Me, and Myself. They cannot see the world bleeding around them and people hurting. They are blind and deaf to the opportunities of being a blessing to GOD's Created beings. They cannot appreciate the blessing their talents and gifts are to the physical world;

they cannot appreciate the beauty of God's Handiwork. For the spiritually blind, the world unfortunately, revolves around their small accomplishments and environment. A spiritually blind person also has spiritual illness. What is that? It means they have an emotional and cognitive malady that arises out of their failure to respond to GOD's love resulting in separation from GOD, from him/herself and from others.

Those who are spiritually blind, may think they have it ALL, but many may find out sooner or later that they DO NOT. They find instead that there is No Rest for the wicked. Many spiritually empty people have a Deep yearning for fulfilling and a satisfying life; they will search in ALL the wrong places but will not find it. Some will resort to the 'Bottle' only to find out, hopefully, before becoming bed-ridden with cirrhosis of the liver, that the bottle was not the answer. No one will find healing from 'the wrong clinic' for it is Only when you visit the correct clinic, and you submit yourself to the "right" surgical knife of the Master Surgeon that true Transplant and Healing will take place. Attending a 'mausoleum' (dead church) does not mean anything; you must know Him and have a relationship with Him. Know Him as your true personal Saviour,

On the other hand, spiritual eyes give you 20/20 vision not prescribed by Dr Ophthalmologist. Those with spiritual eyes can see into the invisible world, like Elijah and Elisha. They can see that the armies of God outnumber the enemy's army. Spiritual 20/20 vision allows us to see the hurting people of the world as God sees them. We can, see that they need a touch from the Saviour for healing, for salvation, for hope and faith. With Spiritual 20/20 vision we can see fully our destiny as we trust and obey. We also see that in spite of persecutions and edicts that our final destination while be a place of hope and peace, with the only light being the presence of our Saviour and God. The author thanks God for hope in the darkness...

GOD said if I (Dr Fair-Brain) suffer or am persecuted for His Name's sake, **"Count it All joy..."** Do you mean, counting it All Joy even with your job position unfairly revoked, with no explanations given and left with Nothing? That is correct; it was very painful, and though I could NOT understand GOD's reason, Divine obedience was required of me. I do not have to like or understand anything. I was reminded that even Storms have an end; they do not last for ever. I am looking back at where the storm caused destruction and have now moved away and to God the glory because I am still alive and well.

I agree the evil one put me through several weeks and months of emotional turmoil.

I might have gone through the thick of the Storm or call it a Night of Despair, the Night of 'NO HOPE' but dawn was coming. It was at this time that I knew and felt the sweet aroma and comfort of my GOD. He said, **"I will be with you in Troubled Times and will give you Peace that passes Understanding"**.

In closing, let me share with you my favourite verse from GOD's WORD which says, "ALL things (Not some things), work TOGETHER for GOOD to them that LOVE GOD..." It might have looked like the adversary had succeeded in pushing me under and things were never going to work out for good for me but there was tomorrow. It is said, "**The First will be LAST and the Last will be FIRST**". I receive and claim it. In GOD's time and timing, I will be up there; I am not saying that is all I am aiming for in life. No! I just want to be a Blessing to God's people. Material wealth is NOT my Goal. I pray that you and I will be happy with our destinations.

Somebody has also said, "**Today's peacocks are tomorrow's feather dusters.**" Right now, I am struggling to locate a job, so I can pay rent, feed my family, and meet other financial obligations. Of course, I do not have to worry because my **Father is Jehovah Jireh**. He has provided for me as He usually did. The enemy may not be pleased to hear that his plans and intentions were not fulfilled.

I will quit trembling and trust; I will stop having sleepless nights and rest in His Promises; I will quit pouting and praise. I will quit worrying and wait on His time, and I will quit struggling and trust and believe in my God.

The reason I write these spiritual Nuggets is for hope. I hope and pray that these words will open the reader's spiritual eyes, and new revelations will begin to heal lives. Spiritual eyes to view life from a different perspective, see the world around them as God sees it, understanding God's patience and compassion for his fallen creation.

Spiritual 20/20 vision also brings joy. JOY is when you put JESUS first, Others next and Yourself last. Joy in Jesus will make you be at peace with even your enemy. Then you can trust and obey the command of God to pray for your enemy. May

GOD open your spiritual eyes and sensitize them to needs of the hurting world.

Chapter #16

RACISM AND HATRED SHOULD NEVER BE TOLERATED AGAIN.

R acism is a pandemic problem caused by ignorance differentiating people with skin colour; and the solution is education. The problem of racism has become serious in every country. Racism might occur in any place like school, hospital, workplace, country and so on.

'Racist' and 'racism' are provocative words in genuinely civilized societies. To some, these words have reached the level of curse words in their offensiveness. Yet, 'racist' and 'racism' are descriptive words of a reality that cannot be denied. **(http:// academic.udayton.edu/race/intro.htm)**

Race issues are so fundamental in the world. For an example, some Caucasians believe that race is the primary determinant of human abilities and capacities. In fact, such individuals respond to people-of-colour (Black) because of race. Therefore, people of different skin colour are injured by judgements or actions that are directly or indirectly racist. In 17th to 18th centuries, the slavery system was common in America. The Black people worked as slaves for the White people. White people insulted them and even abused them. Fortunately, President Abraham Lincoln abolished slavery. Since then, the percentage of discrimination has decreased over the years. Proof? The election of President Barack Obama. **(http://academic.udayton. edu/race/intro.htm)**

Another example, when Portuguese sailors first explored Africa in the 15th and 16th centuries, they came upon empires and cities as advanced as their own and they considered Africans to be serious rivals. Then, there was a match that took place between them; the Portuguese won the match. They began to plunder the continent and forcibly remove its inhabitants to work as slaves. Though the Africans were the indigenous, they were forced into slavery. **This was a definite display of racism (http://www.adl.org/hate-patrol/racism.asp).**

Racial problems have persisted up to this day, in fact there is increase. Racism is experienced throughout the globe. Why does mankind discriminate? This is because of ignorance and their lack of knowledge. Are Black people so different? In fact, the only thing that differentiates us is our skin colour and nothing more. We are all human and we should treat each other equally regardless of our skin colour, race, background, and education. **(http://www.socialpolicy.ca/52100/m17/ m17-t2.stm)**

Institutional Racism

This involves activities which are intended to protect the advantages of a recessive group or conserve or widen the unequal position of a subordinate group; certain structures in society that systematically discriminate against certain groups, such as the former "Apartheid policy" of South Africa or the Jim crow laws in the southern states of America.

Racism in Europe

When we talk about racism, the first-place people we think of is Europe. From the institutionalized racism, especially in colonial times, when racial beliefs were not considered something wrong, to recent times where the effects of neo-Nazism are still felt; Europe has been the cauldron of racism. It has been a complex area with many cultures concentrated in a relatively small area of land. So, it was easy for people in Europe to have conflicts. The conflict of racism arose from erroneous thoughts that each race believed their race was better than others, because of this they would start to insult each other. Besides this, Europe was divided into two groups: the rich and the poor. The rich would discriminate against the poor. For an example, the poor would not be welcome to the high-class restaurants meant for the rich only and neither would the rich have meals with the poor. The rich certainly showed prejudice against the poor. The poor were also most likely to have the higher rate of committing crimes because of this disparity.

(http://www.globalissues.org/article/165/
racism#RacisminEurope)

Racism in Africa

Before most of Africa became independent, there were lots of wars and conflicts between the indigenous people and foreigners. While most of the conflicts have access to natural resources at their core and involve a number of non-African nations and corporation; the conflicts were worsened by stirring up ethnic differences and hatred. In Zimbabwe, there had been increasing racism against the white farmers, due to poverty and lack of land ownership by Africans. The foreigners took over the land in Africa but did not give the Africans job opportunities. The foreigners discriminated against the African aborigine. **They despised the African locals because of their <u>dark black skin colour</u>.** They also thought they were superior and had a higher social status as compared to the African local. Even White missionaries had the same attitude towards the local blacks **(http://www.globalissues.org/article/165/racism#RacisminAfrica).**

At the age of 12 years, I went to live with American White missionaries. I slept in box storage room and on a small rug they used to clean their feet from the rain outside. They paid my school fees, and when I got back from school, I would cut grass around the house with a cycle and water flowers with a horse pipe. I was separated from my mother at that difficult time for dysfunctional family reasons I did not quite understand.

Important result of Racism

"Wars were waged against other humans, violating the most sacred rights of life and autonomy in the persons of a distant people who never offended the attackers, capturing and carrying them into slavery to other distant places, or cause miserable deaths during their transportation there. This heinous warfare and the opprobrium of infidel powers was promoted by the "Christian" King of Great Britain. Determined to keep open a market where men could be bought and sold, he encouraged every legislative attempt not to prohibit or to restrain this execrable commerce.

(http://www.sonofthesouth.net/slavery/history-slavery.htm)

Racism in Today's Society

Racism has always been a serious problem in every country. Although it is the 21st century, the racism problem is still happening everywhere. Racism comes from different cultural values, ethnic backgrounds, as well as the physical appearances. The conflict of racism occurs when the majority group feels that the different cultures and values of the minority group is denigrating the existing society. Racism has been one of the most significant issues that people have had to face and fight, and it is still being faced in our daily lives in places such as in schools, workplaces, and places of residence. Racism can destroy a person without any notice, for it can hurt and discriminate against them in many ways. For an example, the victims of racism will feel life is meaningless and then contemplate suicide, because they are always made to think and feel negatively.

At the present time, there are so many types of people in our world and crimes are always happening around us. If we see a black male standing at a corner during night, we just assume that he is contemplating theft or is involved in a gang or has intentions of committing other types of crimes. **Often, black males are good people, but many may think they are bad guys with bad intentions.** We cannot always determine what type of person by just looking at his face or skin-colour. This is racial stereotyping. There is common saying, **"Never judge a book by its covers…" We should apply that saying to people too:** "Never judge a person by the skin (cover)."

Unfortunately, the media is often responsible for judging by the cover. It happens in the way news is reported. The media makes erroneous statements to the public in the way the news is reported. Here are two examples from two photographs in the newspaper:

#1 One was of a black woman, wading through a flood of water and was carrying a bag full of food and a case of soft drinks. **The article described the picture as a black woman who had just stolen from a local grocery store.**

#2 The other photo showed a white couple, also were wading through a flood of water and also carrying a bag of food and a case of soft drinks. But the author described it as a white couple who had just found food from a local grocery store.

(http://www.nextstepu.com/articlePage1. aspx?timeline=1&artId=2432)

<u>(http://www.bukisa.com/articles/35323 the-effect-of-rac-ism-on-american-prison-population)</u>

In prison people separate themselves and gather with people who resemble them. This is often done according to race and gang affiliations. Living in prison is about survival since many people die while in prison; the goal is to live.

How race is viewed and treated in prisons, generally will spill over into the general population upon release, and that is the sad reality. Instead of promoting racist behaviours and beliefs, prison should serve the purpose of working to rehabilitate the inmates so they can become productive members of society. Prison is a subculture, so **eliminating racism and prejudice in the inmates' habits and thoughts could be the new culture in prison.** Similar to the Hajj of Malcolm X. Everyone one is welcomed to the common community of prison as all are welcomed to the common prison community.

Race is used extensively in police profiling. Racial profiling refers to the use of individuals' features when considering them as suspects of crimes. **The majority of police officers view members of the black and other non-white communities as suspects of major crimes such as drug trafficking.** In such cases, colour makes members of the minority community prime suspects for crimes. For members of the minority communities, "guilty until proven innocent" is the rule that governs them. **In my opinion, George Floyd in the USA is recent example to date.**

The racial disproportionate prison population is not only caused by police profiling but also by unfair criminal and punishment policies. This is witnessed in professional jobs where Black people are assumed to be incapable and incompetent of making professional personnel capable of making reasonable decisions such as doctors or nurses making sensible clinical decisions on their own (Dr Fair-Brain).

The War on Drugs, for instance, is seen by many not as a war against illicit drugs but as a war against the black community. Many blacks are incarcerated behind bars (some innocently). Many have suffered severe punishment due to this War; and its accompanying racial differential policies such as the Anti-Drug Abuse Act of 1998 in the USA. According to this Act, individuals convicted of possessing and dealing in powder cocaine receive a lesser punishment than individuals convicted of possessing and dealing in crack cocaine. (http://www.bukisa.com/articles/35323_the-effect-of-racism-on-american-prison-population)

The mandatory minimum sentence meted against individuals dealing in 50 grams of crack cocaine is ten years while the same mandatory minimum sentence is meted against individuals dealing in 5000 grams of powder cocaine. Racism appears to be the motivation anti-drug abuse act, because most individuals arrested for crack cocaine-related charges are predominantly Black. Whereas majority of individuals arrested for powder cocaine-related crimes are predominantly White. As a result, blacks suffer harsher punishments than their white counterparts despite committing a similar crime.

Racism significantly impacts inmates convicted of homicide in a number of ways. The race of the homicide victim, perpetrator, jurors, defendants, and prosecutors play significant roles in determining the kind of sentences that will be passed to convicted murders. Research shows that **in states where capital punishment is legal, the punishment is more frequently used in cases where the victim of a homicide is White than when the victim is Black or a member of other minority communities.** In addition, capital punishment is used more often when the perpetrator of a homicide is a member of a minority group than when he or she is White.

The effect of racism on the prison population can only be minimized if participation of members of the minority communities in the criminal justice system is increased. This will provide minorities with equal protection and defence as that offered to the whites. **(http://www.helium.com/items/1293570-effect-of-racism-on-american-prison-population)**

"Solution" for the Pandemic Racism

People from all people's groups, are asking the question, **"what do we with pandemic racism?"** That is a question which needs to be answered. The question needs to be addressed now not tomorrow. How do we do it without being drawn into a destructive response? History teaches us, righteous and peaceful protests must be encouraged, voices must speak up and those in authority must listen and respond accordingly, with gentleness.

Together, we can effectuate positive change if we pursue it with wisdom, tenacity, and resolve. We need tangible recommendations on what we all can do right now; to bring about a reversal of injustices, racial evils and promote healing in our world.

People have been talking about racism for centuries, yet people continue to be racists. How do we solve this problem? Everybody has dealt with it, politicians, spiritual leaders, community activities, yet the problem of racism persists. **I believe the reason is lack of collective global research for the solution or what I term <u>"Vaccine to the Pandemic of Racism"</u>.**

First, we must admit that racism is a problem and that it is a psycho-social problem. Racism is like alcoholism; the people must admit they have a problem. Admit they are out of control; **The problem with racism and racialism is that many people are in denial.**

Next, we can debate racial issues for an example, we can discuss this problem at school with teachers or friends or parents. This action can help us get more information about racism.

Additionally, we should acknowledge that all races are capable of intolerance and bigotry. **We need to be indoctrinated that character, not skin colour makes the person.**

We all need to reflect on what has become a volatile issue after the accidental death of Mr George Floyd in America; the upsurge of racism in our own country, when Britain voted to leave the EU, the POSK in West London had xenophobic graffiti scrawled across its doors.

We must say this is simply not acceptable in a humane society, and that it should never be provoked or promoted. We need to grasp again our basic sense of purpose; in living together, creating together and fashioning a society together. It is that sense of purpose that we may have lost focus of; believing that the purpose of politics is to manipulate power; the purpose of business is simply to make profit. This challenge has been with us for a while now. Our purpose must be our common good, the good of all with no one excluded. Our politicians must deal with their issues, businessmen and banks with their issues, but the fundamental purpose is to build a world in which strength is used for service and no one is excluded.

"The great challenge for those leading the nation now is to speak for everyone.

Racism is Discriminating. I have lived my life with racial problems; and grew up in an area with mostly people of my race. However, it always seemed to me that people who were not my race behaved terribly whenever it came to dealing with us (Blacks). However, **the Caucasian people generally have always been very rude about the black people's behaviour; saying they are too loud, they are lazy, they believe the world owes them something and those who worked hard to be competitive in the world market are dubbed as a mistake.** The author of this book, a **professional man (Dr Fair-Brain), was made to feel as if he did not belong in the group of professionals because of his colour (Black) and his ethnic background.**

Every joke and every snide remark had to do with a "Nigger" or "Coloured or Kaffir" or "black ignoramus". The Asians and the Indians are not spared either. They are labelled by certain derogatory terms or how they smell, or Indian accents, and it feels as if they are mocking something over which they have no control. There are all bad habits, and a discouragement to cultural growth and to living together as a people. Name calling and racial slurs are negative and toxic language because racist talk makes the person, at whom the racist language is directed, feel negative (sad, angry, frustrated, disgusted) and like a second-class citizen. Therefore, if one is repeatedly being racist, it should not be tolerated.

For those of you who use "freedom of speech" as an excuse to continue racism. How ridiculous! Civilized people are not vulgar or profane, instead they are kind and humane people; they are considerate of people's feelings. Civilized people are mature and smart people; they should be peaceful, welcoming, tolerant, and understanding. Racism leads to hatred and this hurts people. Hatred hurts a civil society.

Racial discrimination is illegal. Why not racism?

They took cigarette ads off TV because smoking had been proven to cause cancer. Racial discrimination is already illegal, so why is advocating for racist beliefs not illegal? Why not remove legitimacy from racism, by making advocating for racism illegal and punishable by law?

Racism is incipient criminality, punish it harshly

You would not be punishing a very elevated class of people, you would be punishing cowards and bullies, the kind of people who will always do the wrong thing unless they are whacked with a big stick. Those people who do not want racism to be punished with law, may be afraid that they are racists themselves. Too bad, if you are a racist, it does not matter if you are nice in all other things, you are a social offender and you need to be punished with stiff fines at the very least. I cannot stand racists of any race, colour, or creed, they should be punished equally worldwide until this obnoxious and pernicious problem is stopped! You cannot coddle them, but rather treat them the way they treat others. You will never stop This problem will never until it is harshly attacked. Give no excuses, there are none! Enough is enough with this ugly anti-social lifestyle, it has to be dealt with harshly and sternly. **Racism must go; we are the idiots if we let it continue forever! Concerned with freedom of speech? Freedom of speech must not violate rights of other people.**

Racism and Hatred must Never be Tolerated

We all need to reflect on what has been a volatile topic for many years and ponder what is needed now. "Firstly, I am very conscious of the mixing of people of different races in the world as a whole has become inevitable. Racism, and requisite hatred towards each other is something we must not tolerate. We must simply not accept racism in a humane society, and it should never be provoked or promoted. "Racism and hatred must never be tolerated, but there is no need for fear.

We have an important job in defining the boundaries where we live. Then and only then will the values we seek to live and to promote be attainable. We must see ourselves living in the presence of God, living with that transcendent boundary. Once that transcendent dimension is simply put to one side, then there is no space to see ourselves under the providence of God; and living consciously in the presence of God Without a transcendent boundary, society closes in on itself and becomes much more self-centred and much more divided. We need to grasp again our basic sense of purpose; in living together, creating together, and fashioning a society. It is that sense of purpose that we may have lost focus of; believing that the purpose of politics is to manipulate power; the purpose of business is simply to make profit for a few. This challenge has been with us for a long time now.

Our purpose must be our common good, the good of all with no one excluded. Our politicians must deal with their issues, businessmen and banks with their issues, but the fundamental purpose is to build a world in which strength is used for service and no one is excluded or discriminated because of their origin, colour, or ethnic background. I believe that every leader needs to reflect on our failure to listen and to give voice to those who are voiceless. The great challenge for those leading the nations now is to speak for everyone to care for everyone.

GOD Loves Everyone; Racism is Manufactured Hatred.

Have you ever noticed that racism is a learned behaviour? Racism is taught. Think about this: if while a person is raised, they see everyone being treated the same and never see a person judged by their skin colour this is how they will view the world being colour blind to race. If you are taught that a person with a different skin tone is inferior to you, then you might believe this. As a child the lessons we are taught tend to stick on you the rest of your life. Do you have memories? As a child you played with any kid without ever putting any thought into skin colour, into a person's race.

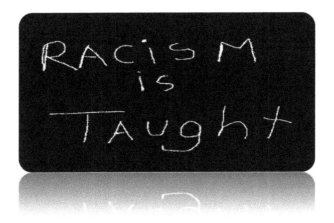

Racism is taught in the homes

The term race does not appear in the Bible. The Bible refers to differing peoples in terms such as family, tribe, people, and nation. It groups people according to familial relationships and then into nationalities. **Nowhere in the Bible is prejudice based on what we determine as Race, i.e., colour of hair, skin, eyes, or physical characteristics.** When God commanded the children of Israel to be a separated people or to destroy other peoples, it was always based upon the principle of separation from sin. The same principle of separation is presented in the

New Testament when Christians are commanded to come out of the world and not be unequally yoked with the unsaved. (2 Cor. 6:14).

But you have most probably heard of 'white' professing men-of-God talk about a couple being unequally yoked if their skin colours were different. That is pure heresy and is unacceptable in the ecumenical chambers of heaven.

In Scripture, there are several references to problems in which people with different racial backgrounds were involved. In each case, the instruction is clear that God made no distinction between races regarding salvation or blessing. **In Numbers 12:1-16, Miriam and Aaron openly criticized Moses for marrying an Ethiopian woman. However, the issue was not racial, but jealousy over Moses' leadership, and the criticism was over marrying a foreigner, any foreigner, and not because she was an Ethiopian (see Number 12:2).** In Acts 13:1 we read of "Simeon that was called Niger" and "Luis of Cyrene". Simeon was also referred to by his Latin name "Niger" which translates as "black" in English). **Racism is not taught in the Bible. Racism is not from God; racism is from Satan.**

Racism and its Effect on Society

Throughout world history, governments have violated and ignored the human and civil rights of their citizens. In some instances, they demonstrated this disregard through customs, etiquette, and racial caste systems that denied human dignity and respect. In most cases, in addition to these customs, segregation rules and laws were established.

Governments ("Nazism") have also endorsed the extermination (ethnic cleansing) of entire classes or races of people. Racism is devastating to a country and its culture. **Racism causes tremendous moral, cultural, and economic suffering to a country and to the world.** When the seeds of hatred and ethnocentrism are planted and fostered in society, it negatively affects every area of life.

"Jim Crow" set the tone in America.

In a relevant example, white supremacy in America extends over centuries, and even the abolition of slavery could not end racism. Instead, it permeated throughout society in other ways in a racial caste system known as "Jim Crow".

More than a set of laws, it was a way of life that kept people of colour from exercising their rights as full citizens. **Jim Crow sent a message that whites were superior to other races, particularly the black race, in all ways, including behaviour, intelligence, morality, and social status. The laws were so pervasive that they regulated every aspect of life, including socialization, sexual relations, marriage, housing, education, entertainment, use of public facilities, and voting rights.**

Those that took a stand against white supremacy risked threats, intimidation, violence, and murder. Legalized racism from federal and state governments continued in the United States until the late 1960s. Yet, even in the 21st century, legislators continue to pass racially discriminatory laws as evidenced by the 200+ segregation cases the Department of Justice is currently pursuing, and violence, intimidation and murder are still the order of the day in America. The United Kingdom, Europe and the rest of the world are no different. The George Floyd insurrections are evidence of continual off shoots of racial hatred and discrimination.

When Racism is Allowed to Thrive

Racism does not allow for a collective contribution of its citizens, which is a critical component of a country's development and success. If a class of people is not allowed to be educated, they cannot make important contributions to society in technological, economical, and medical arenas. The denial of quality education to certain groups of people only serves to obstruct the economic progress of a nation.

The treatment of certain professionals in the United Kingdom based on colour is absurd and barbaric in today's society. Any discrimination or racial injustice mentioned in the NHS Hospitals usually involved those professionals of colour like <u>Dr Gordon Fair-Brain</u> who cried to the top of his voice for help but was not heard because of selective hearing by the people in authority who could have made the difference, all because he was Black in colour.

If a class of people is not allowed to participate culturally, we fail to understand and appreciate our differences and similarities. We become increasingly ethnocentric. We fail to develop socially, unable to get along with our fellow man. No matter how hard a society might try to separate classes or races, the bottom line is that, eventually, we will, at least on some occasions, share the same space. Therefore, it is imperative that we are accepting, not merely tolerant, of others. The connotation for tolerance is that one must acknowledge the other, whereas acceptance encourages complete participation and fellowship. **Today, even the church I went to here in the UK, I noticed the same principle of <u>tolerance</u> and <u>not acceptance</u> among the members of the congregation which is ungodly and hypocritical before Almighty God.**

Racism destroys our morality. No matter what a person's culture or religious belief, racism is based on hypocrisy. To illustrate this point, the Christians have a commandment, issued by Jesus, to "love your neighbour as you love yourself." Most religions have similar philosophies governing their social morality. Yet, there is the hypocrisy going on in the nights with the extremists demonstrate who they really are by burning crosses or participating in hate crimes. **Racism is powerful enough to undermine their Golden Rule and turn it upside down.**

Many times, we, as societies and individuals, think that racism will dissipate on its own; so, we ignore it, repeatedly. And what happens is that some people continue to suffer. <u>**When a black doctor loses his job because white nurses do NOT like the colour of his skin, a nation has not progressed much.**</u> In 1963, Martin Luther King, Jr., made a profound statement in his "Letter from Birmingham Jail":

"When you suddenly find your tongue twisted and your speech stammering as you seek to explain to your six-year old daughter why she can't go to the public amusement park that has just been advertised on television, and see the tears welling up in her eyes when she is told that "Fun-town is closed to 'coloured'

(black) children, and see ominous clouds of inferiority beginning to form in her little mental sky, and see her beginning
to distort her personality by developing an unconscious bitterness toward white people, you will understand why we find
it difficult to wait (for change)."

Dr Fair-Brain is black and a British citizen. He rushed his
wife to an Accident &Emergency department of one NHS
Hospital because of a severe food allergy (Anaphylaxis) and
while in in the department he tried to inquire from the doctor
attending to his wife. At first, **he tried to push the doctor aside
until he learnt that Dr Fair-Brain was also a doctor who had
worked at the same hospital in the Oncology department.**
Though this other doctor did not apologise, Dr Fair-Brain
noticed that the A&E doctor was more friendly and forth
coming. He tried to explain what treatment he had ordered
for his wife and what Dr Fair-Brain could expect as the outcome. Poor doctor! He struggled with the English language so
badly that Dr Fair-Brain had to ask the attending nurse if his
wife had received certain Antihistamines that he knew would
be helpful in putting out the fire of anaphylaxis quickly.

An English nurse finally explained to Dr Fair-Brain what was
going on and what had been done. **On his way home, Dr Fair-
Brain could not help but think that these were the white doctors working in the firing line (A&E) but could Not even
explain themselves.** Surely this doctor had a serious problem
with the language, but he was "White" and the GMC granted
him permission to work because despite his problem, **he had
the most important qualification (White) according to
GMC, but a Black British doctor is actually removed from**

practising because some "White" racial nurses who said the "Black" doctor was not good enough, <u>he was not White.</u> And you still claim racism was over? God help us!

Dr Martin Luther King's message is so clear: "**Racism is most damaging to the children in the society in which they live. The pathology is dehumanization. The cure is humanism**". He also said, "**Darkness cannot drive out darkness, only Light can do that. Hate cannot drive out Hate, Only Love can do that**". Our world is being destroyed, not by the bad people, but by the good and wise people who are content to do nothing.

What the Future Holds

"The issues of American slavery, segregation, and discrimination cannot be viewed within their own individual time capsules. To gain proper perspective, these issues must be viewed collectively as devastating to our culture and threatening to democracy." (<u>Lugo, 2014.</u>)

The United Kingdom is not any better, in case you are quick to point your fingers to the 'American problems' that is not affecting us here. Consider the "Wind Rush", Polish children born in the UK denied citizenship and Polish people being stabbed for just being Polish though white is the colour of their skin.

No one claims to have the ultimate answer or a cure for racism. Evidently, neither does the world around me since racism raises its ugly head more times than one can count and, in more ways, than one can imagine. Even one act is intolerable for us. One cannot regulate thought or feeling through legislation. Only certain actions can be regulated, like the assurance of voting rights, the dismantling of racist policies, and punishment for those who perpetuate violent attacks and commit civil rights violations. It is especially hurtful when institutions you think should be well informed are the same ones which seem to condone racial hatred, and many of the repugnant atrocities.

It may be bold to say that sometimes legislation serves to hide racism. People will find a way to practice it. For example, an employer could still feasibly say one person is more qualified than another but could be favouring one race over another. The Isle of Wight had nothing concrete against Dr Fair-Brain but had to uphold the fabricated allegations by a few "white racists" who claimed the doctor was NOT competent enough. When the basis, for the claims, by "white" nurses was rendered invalid, they fabricated other lies which were convincing to the Disciplinary Committee made up of White officers who investigated the allegations aimed at derailing the Black doctor.

Laws cannot prosecute people who curse the air blue and shout racial slurs at NHS staff; but quick to discipline you for verbalizing Christian messages of encouragements. A consultant from the Accident and Emergency room, supposed to be the Responsible Officer for the Acute Oncology Service, cursed the air blue and sometimes at his colleague, Dr Fair-Brain. Was he chastised for it? No. Who condemned it? After all he was a White consultant. Nobody corrected him.

It is our sincere hope (the people) that one day, little by little, humanity will learn from the many tragedies that have been perpetuated in the name of racism. The rise of multicultural education is a great way to start. We need to understand the psychological, historical, and individualistic dynamics of racism first and then encourage others to take a stand against it publicly.

It serves no purpose to claim to believe in something and not have the courage to practice it. It serves no purpose to limit anti-racism by one's refusal to participate in racial acts, because it shows a lack of responsibility and ownership in one's community. To combat racism, we must be bold and persistent. We must take a stand and make a commitment to ourselves, our children, and our society to oppose racism when we see it, and to seek for ways to eliminate it. The human community cannot afford to lose one more person to the evils of racism.

We must Not tolerate RACISM.

"We all have a part to play in stopping racism" the doctor says. "It goes alongside bullying, mobbing and abuse. We should not tolerate it." We must all say, "No, that is not right. Do not tease that person. Do not laugh at their jokes. Do not pick on or make fun of that person." We should all say this wherever and whenever necessary.

I know it seems like you are going over the top, but it must start somewhere. Even if it is just a word, do not let it go by. If you see a weed, you pluck it out right away so, you must stop it from spreading. You have to keep at it, work on it, even if people think you are becoming a pain."

Because of her faith, Mrs Willard, a strong believer in Christ, refuses to allow negativity to take hold after she lost one of her sons to racism.

"We do not want to be eaten up with bitterness," she says. "We are Christians and believe we should love, not hate. I have seen what bitterness can do to people. Who does it harm? Oneself. We are already in pain. Why make it any worse?"

She is surprised that other people are in awe of her forbearance. "All I am trying to do is live by the word of God. The commandment says, "Love your neighbour…" For us, it is not just words on pages; we give those words life; we lift them from the page. It gives us strength.

Racism should Not be Tolerated in a workplace.

We close this discussion on Racism on one situation that happened in my country of origin.

"A 'kaffir' (ignorant black person) must not tell me what to do" – Racism and hate-speech at a workplace in Azania (South Africa).

It was similar to what happened to Dr Fair-Brain at the Isle of "White" where the 'White' nurses felt they would not be led by a black man and from the "dark continent" and the Trust acted as if they were not aware of what these two nurses meant without verbalizing it. Institutional racism is still existent at all Trusts in the United Kingdom like it or not.

In a landmark constitutional court decision, the court expressed itself clearly on racism at work – in the context of an employee uttering the words 'I can't understand how k*ffirs think' and 'A k*ffir must not tell me what to do.' (A white man was telling their black boss.)

The employee was an Azanian official with 25 years' service. The 'Boer' (White man) had an altercation with his superior (Black) and referred to him as a kaffir. A disciplinary enquiry was convened, and he pleaded guilty. The chairperson did not dismiss him but gave him a final written warning and a two-week punitive suspension; plus, he was ordered to attend counselling. The Azanian Commissioner changed the sanction to that of dismissal, without giving the employee a chance to argue that he should not be dismissed. The employee took the case to the Higher Authorities and won. He was reinstated into his position. The Commissioner took the matter to the Labour Court. From there it went to the Labour Appeal Court and finally ended up in the Constitutional Court, where the Commissioner fought not to have to give the employee his job back. SARS appears to have conceded that they should have given the employee a chance to defend himself against the sanction of dismissal before it was substituted for the lesser sanction that had been imposed by the disciplinary chairperson. The only issue for the Constitutional Court to decide therefore was whether reinstatement was the appropriate sanction.

The Azanian Commissioner argued that racism in the workplace was an extremely serious issue, and that as an organ of state it had a special constitutional obligation to protect and promote employees' rights to equality and human dignity,

which racism violates. Thus, they could not take the employee back into the workforce after he had 'hurled the k*ffir insult' at his colleague.

The Constitutional Court agreed and held that by saying that 'A k*ffir must not tell me what to do,' the employee had impugned the intellectual capacity, leadership, and managerial abilities of all of his African co-workers. He had expressed the view that that they were not worthy of exercising authority over him. He had displayed the worst kind of contempt, racism and insubordination towards Africans and his remarks were grossly offensive and 'dignity-suffocating'. This meant that it was completely inappropriate for him to return to the workplace.

Dismissal was the only proper sanction for him. To let him return to work when his African co-employees knew that he had called one of them a k*ffir and that he regarded them as lazy, incapable of leading him and intellectually inferior to him solely because of their race would be like 'recklessly leaving a ticking time-bomb unattended to, knowing that it could self-detonate at any time with consequences that are too ghastly to contemplate.' In addition to the problems in the workplace, the enormous problems that racism causes in the country at large must also be factored into the equation. The Commissioner, as an organ of state, has an especially important role to fight against racism and to eradicate it wherever it appears.

The Constitutional Court said that there might be exceptional circumstances where an employee need not face the harshest sanction for using the word 'k*ffir' in the workplace – but it emphasised that such cases would be rare indeed and that the presumption would be that a continued employment relationship would be intolerable, and that the employee should be dismissed. The court said that the word 'k*ffir' was the 'worst of all racial vitriols a white person (could) ever direct at an African in this country' and that it 'captures the heartland of racism (and) its contemptuous disregard and dignity-nullifying effect on others.' As such, conduct like that of the Azanian Commission employee must always be dealt with fairly but firmly. Mollycoddling does not cut it, said the court, it is hate speech and it must be rooted out of society and the workplace.

This echoes the words of the Labour Appeal Court in 2002 when it said that 'The attitude of those who refer to, or call, Africans as "k*ffirs" is an attitude that should have no place in any workplace in this country (Azania) and should be rejected with absolute contempt by all those in our country – black and white – who are committed to the values of human dignity, equality and freedom that now form the foundation of our society.'

TOGETHER as ONE Human Race Under One GOD!

Chapter # 17

FINAL WORD: EXCERPTS FROM THE WISDOM OF DR MARTIN L. KING, JR.

The persistence of racism throughout the world at large remains a serious challenge to the hope of mankind. Racism challenges the most cherished values of liberty and justice.

Continued incidents which stir up racial tensions, remind us that Hatred and Animosity are still pandemic. News events repeatedly remind us of the tenuous and fragile nature of racial harmony in the world. Regularly we hear of incident after incident in different parts of the world. Years after the passing of Dr King, black people are being thrown out of China because they are being accused of having brought the COVID-19. How ridiculous! It is nothing other than racism. **These are the things that continue to fan the fires of racism throughout the world.**

Tolerance has no cohesive nor healing power. It means more than leaving one another alone. It is like placing a band aid on a festering wound. It leads to indifference, not understanding. Tolerance allows the gulfs between us to remain in place. In fact, there is little in the concept of tolerance to pull us away from racial isolation.

Tolerance brings with it an implicit moral relativism. Who is to say what is right and what is wrong? Moral relativism suggests that there are no absolutes to which we can all be held account- able. Such a thing was far from the thinking of the Man of God himself – Martin Luther King. In one of his works Dr King makes the following statements:

"At the centre of the Christian Faith is the affirmation that there is a God in the universe who is the ground and essence of all reality. A being of infinite love and boundless power, God is the Creator, Sustainer, and Conserver of values. In contrast to ethical rela- tivism, Christianity sets forth a system of absolute moral values and affirms that God has placed within the very structure of this universe certain moral principles that are fixed and immutable.

Dr King did not speak in terms of tolerance, his ideal was love. **"Hate cannot drive out Hate, only Love can do that."**

In current discussions of race relations, the word Love is seldom mentioned. Dr King insisted love was the dominant or critical value by which we could overcome racial strife.

The love Dr King spoke of was the God kind of love, one that is unconditional, unselfish and seeks the absolute good of another party. That kind of love is a tough love, one that confronts wrong and injustice with the truth – absolute truth as decreed by an All-powerful God and enables the individual to love their enemy.

Martin Luther King's Dream

As we consider giving new life to "The Dream" we must acknowledge that, in Dr King's speaking and writing. "The Dream" does begin with God, there is no other absolute transcendent truth on which to base a call to justice. Nor is there any source from which to draw the strength to love about which he spoke. Too often, those who claim to be Christians have failed to live in keeping with the clear teachings of the Christian Scriptures. These failures have frequently been in matters of race.

Dr King's Call to a Genuine Relationship with God

Dr King's life was devoted to challenging the American nation to live out a more consistent obedience to the moral absolutes of the Scriptures. His repeated plea was for men and women to enter the kind of personal relationship with God that transcended that which could be seen and that which was being experienced. Hear Dr King as he spoke to the men and women who contended that God was unnecessary or irrelevant to our modern lives:

"At times we may feel that we do not need God, but on the day when the storms of disappointment rage, the winds of disaster blow, and the tidal waves of grief beat against our

lives, if we do not have a deep and pillar of faith, our emotional lives will be ripped to shreds."

"There is so much frustration in the world because we have relied on other gods rather than the Almighty GOD. We have diverted our attention to the gods of science and pleasure only to find that gave us the atomic bomb, Sodom, and Gomorrah, produced fears and anxieties that science and pleasure can never mitigate.

We have worshiped the god of pleasure only to discover that thrills play out and sensations are short-lived. We have bowed before the god of money only to discover that there are such things as love and friendship that money cannot buy; and that in a world of possible depressions stock markets crash, and bad business investments, money is a rather uncertain deity.

"These transitory gods are not able to save us or bring lasting happiness to the human heart. Only God, Almighty, can do this. It is Faith in Him that we must rediscover. With this faith, we can transform bleak and desolate valleys into sunlit paths of joy and bring new light into the dark caverns of pessimism." (Strength to Love)

Is it Possible to End Racism in the world?

Like me, are you discouraged about the prospect of us never overcoming the Pandemic Racial evil that still permeates this world? Or are you frustrated by your inability to genuinely love others who are different from you especially those who always seem to claim they are God's chosen race (the Whites)? Dr

King recommended Faith in Jesus Christ of Nazareth as the antidote for this seemingly incurable malady.

Evil can be cast out, not by man alone nor by a dictatorial God who invades our lives, but when we open the door and invite Him through Christ to enter. "Behold, I stand at the door, and knock; if any man hears my voice, and open the door; I will come into him, and will sup with him, and he with me." God is too courteous to break open the door, but when we open it in faith believing, a divine and human confrontation will transform our sin-ruined lives into radiant personalities." (Strength to Love).

What can Change a Heart of Racism

A relationship with God gives us the power to overcome whatever sin we may be struggling with, including the sin of Racism. Racism stands not only as a barrier between people, but as an offense between us and God. The reason Dr King could recommend Christ as a solution to the problem of racism is Jesus' death on the cross which paid the price for all our sins. He then rose from the dead and now offers us the forgiveness of God and the power to live new lives. Dr King put it this way:

"Man is a sinner in need of God's forgiving grace. This is not deadening pessimism; it is Christian realism." (Strength to Love)

Our need for Jesus is truly the great equalizer of the races. We all are sinners in need of a Saviour. We all stand before God, not based on one race's superiority over another, morally, culturally, financially, politically, or in any other way.

Evil can be cast out, not by man alone nor by a dictatorial God who invades our lives, but when we open the door and invite God through Christ to enter." —MLK

All the races of the world, all the cultures of the world, need the same Saviour. His name is Jesus Christ.

What Martin Luther King described as our need for a **"divine and human confrontation"** is offered at God's initiative. It requires that we place our faith in what Jesus did as our own personal payment for sin and inviting Him to enter our lives "when we open the door and invite God through Christ to enter."

Dr King's words still ring true today. We can give new life to "The Dream," following the path of Dr King. Our path may not lead to martyrdom by an assassin's bullet as it did for Dr Martin Luther King, but it does lead to dying to our selfish ways and self-sufficiency.

Such a faith is not a weak-kneed, escapist religious exercise, but a courageous pursuit of that which is ultimately good, right, and true.

"In his magnanimous love, God freely offers to do for us that we cannot do for ourselves. Our humble and openhearted acceptance is faith. So, by faith we are saved. Man filled with God and God operating through man bring unbelievable changes in our individual and social lives." (Strength to Love)

"The Dream" starts with God as revealed through His Son, Jesus Christ. Through a relationship with Him, we can be agents of healing in a world that is sick with racial and ethnic conflict. As God transforms our lives, we have the potential to embody that which Martin Luther King dreamed…an end to racism in America and the rest of the world.

Racism runs deep. It can seem like an insurmountable task to overcome institutional racism, and it can be unsettling to confront racist tendencies within yourself. Do not think that you need to do it alone. Find your voice, educate yourself, and speak up about the injustice that you encounter. Be bold and act with intention.

Dealing with Day-to-Day Racism

Intervene. Do not take racism lying down. Act on your beliefs when you come across injustice, prejudice, and discriminatory words. Call out racism when you see it. Do not be afraid to stand up for someone who is being mistreated! Use your words, your actions, and your influence. Be bold but be smart. Think about how you can intervene most effectively. Violence is not the answer.

Document injustice. Keep a cell phone camera handy and take video footage of any oppressive acts that you encounter. Do not be afraid to videotape law enforcement officers if you feel that they are physically or verbally oppressing a civilian. **Broadcast the truth. Show your friends, tell your story, and post your footage to social media. If you cannot take video, take photos, or record audio.** At the very least, pay close attention. This may explain why Dr Fair-Brain has written the book, to tell my story. A solid eyewitness account is better than nothing. The **intention of this book is to try and expose some of the truths and evils of RACISM.**

Keep a level head. React with intention, and advocate non-violence. Try to hold your cool and maintain perspective in the face of deep injustice. Do not submit but be careful about acting with anger. Sometimes, it is best to slow down and consider the wisest way to react.

Take your cues from nonviolent activists like Rosa Parks, Nelson Mandela, Harriet Tubman, Dr Gordon Fair-Brain and Martin Luther King, Jr.: men and women who used their frustration to help people rather than hurt people. Each day be the change that you wish to see in the world. Consider that anger often arises in response to anger. Ask yourself whether, by reacting angrily, you will solve the problem – or only feed the cycle of anger.

Placing Racism in Context

Understand why people look different. The history of humanity is the story of people that, over tens of thousands of years, migrated from the jungles and savannas of Africa into Europe and the vast sweep of Asia; navigated ships through the islands of Polynesia using the currents and the stars; followed the hunt from Siberia, across the frozen-over Bering Strait, into the wild heart of North America; and spread, by roughly 10,000 years ago, across the whole grand span of the Americas – to the tip of Tierra del Fuego. Everywhere that our ancestors went, some people stayed, and some people eventually moved on. The people that stayed adapted to their environment in various ways: people in cold northern climes, with less sunlight, developed lighter hair and skin, while people living nearer the equator tended to produce more melanin to protect their skin from the heat.

Look past these superficial differences at the underlying DNA. From South Africa to Siberia, Bangladesh to Brazil, Canada to Kazakhstan: we are all genetically homo sapiens. We are all human, and God Only created One Human Race.

It goes without saying that Dr T Gordon Fair-Brain Mtetwa, as a Black Man, was not only failed by the United Kingdom Health Care system, but his overall treatment was grossly offensive and dignity-suffocating; he was a victim of deliberate hatred and discrimination with gross infringement of his human and inalienable rights. The NHS Trust did not care to investigate the report of 'Racism' against the doctor and why a sudden report against him was taken straight to the Chief Medical Officer (CMO) before his Clinical Director (CD) was informed during the two to three months of being at the Isle of "White" Trust. He was made to be intellectually inferior, without any basis, simply because of his God-given Colour (Black). The Trust's CMO and CD were careless and clearly showed they condoned the behaviour of the two "White Racial" Nurses. The behaviour of other Trusts involved, and the GMC were highly reprehensible and unacceptable.

THE EPILOGUE:

The word terrorism is on our lips daily because of the heinous crimes and destruction associated with it, yet Racism has caused more damage whether covertly or overtly. Racism involves prejudice, discrimination, or antagonism directed against someone of a different race based on the belief that one's own race is superior.

"Hating people because of their colour/race is wrong. And it does not matter which colour does the hating. It's just plainly wrong." – Muhammed Ali

The hatred directed toward others simply for being of a different race, colour and religion has been the focus of many wars and minor military conflicts. "Racism is still alive and among us, but it is up to us to prepare our children for what they have to meet, and, hopefully, we shall overcome." This statement was made by Rosa Parks in 1998. While some may say that this took place a long time ago, **racism and the mentality of white supremacy is still very much alive in modern days. It is an unstoppable pandemic evil.**

Aluta continua (the struggle continues)

Dr T. Gordon Fair-Brain Mtetwa, BA, MD, MSc.
& Diploma in Clinical Oncology.

CPSIA information can be obtained
at www.ICGtesting.com
Printed in the USA
LVHW012326130522
718654LV00007B/16